The Faerie Queene

Open Guides to Literature

Series Editor: Graham Martin (Professor of Literature, The Open University)

Titles in the Series

GARETH ROBERTS

The Faerie Queene

Open University Press
Buckingham · Philadelphia

To my aunt, Olga Howell

Open University Press
Celtic Court
22 Ballmoor
Buckingham
MK18 1XW

and
1900 Frost Road, Suite 101
Bristol, PA 19007, USA

First Published 1992

A catalogue record of this book is available from the British Library

Library of Congress Cataloging-in-Publication Data

Roberts, Gareth, 1949-
   The Faerie queene/Gareth Roberts.
     p. cm. – (Open guides to literature)
   Includes bibliographical references and index.
   ISBN 0-335-09036-2 (hb). – ISBN 0-335-09037-0
   1. Spenser, Edmund, 1552?–1599. Faerie queene. I. Title.
II. Series.
   PR2358:R59 1992
   821'.3 – dc20
                                             91-43028
                                               CIP

Typeset by Best-set Typesetter Ltd, Hong Kong
Printed in Great Britain by St Edmundsbury Press Ltd,
Bury St Edmunds, Suffolk

Contents

Series Editor's Preface

The intention of this series is to provide short introductory books about major writers, texts, and literary concepts for students of courses in Higher Education which substantially or wholly involve the study of Literature.

The series adopts a pedagogic approach and style similar to that of Open University material for Literature courses. *Open Guides* aim to inculcate the reading 'skills' which many introductory books in the field tend, mistakenly, to assume that the reader already possesses. They are, in this sense, 'teacherly' texts, planned and written in a manner which will develop in the reader the confidence to undertake further independent study of the topic. They are 'open' in two senses. First, they offer a three-way tutorial exchange between the writer of the *Guide*, the text or texts in question, and the reader. They invite readers to join in an exploratory discussion of texts, concentrating on their key aspects and on the main problems which readers, coming to the texts for the first time, are likely to encounter. The flow of a *Guide* 'discourse' is established by putting questions for the reader to follow up in a tentative and searching spirit, guided by the writer's comments, but not dominated by an over-arching and single-mindedly-pursued argument or evaluation, which itself requires to be 'read'.

Guides are also 'open' in a second sense. They assume that literary texts are 'plural', that there is no end to interpretation, and that it is for the reader to undertake the pleasurable task of discovering meaning and value in such texts. *Guides* seek to provide, in compact form, such relevant biographical, historical and cultural information as bears upon the reading of the text, and they point the reader to a selection of the best available critical discussions of it. They are not in themselves concerned to propose, or to counter, particular readings of the texts, but rather to put *Guide* readers in a position to do that for themselves. Experienced travellers learn to dispense with guides, and so it should be for readers of this series.

This *Open Guide* to The *Faerie Queene* is best studied in conjunction with the Penguin edition edited by Thomas P. Roche Jr (Harmondsworth 1978).

Graham Martin

Acknowledgements

I suspect that my greatest debts are to students at Exeter University from whose discussions in tutorials on the *Faerie Queene* I have 'borrowed' many of the ideas in this book. My conscious debts are to colleagues in the Classics Department at Exeter, especially Peter Wiseman, who helped me with my small Latin and almost non-existent Greek, and to Josephine McDonagh, Jane Spencer and Michael Wood for giving me impromptu tutorials on aspects of critical theory. I am particularly grateful to Lawrence Normand for reading and always improving drafts of this book, and to Graham Martin for temperately combining patience and rigour as an editor. I would like to hold them all responsible for any signs of '*Errours* endlesse traine' in this book, but I have to acknowledge that that responsibility is mine.

The author and publisher are grateful for the following permissions to reprint copyright material: Dante (1955) *The Divine Comedy: Purgatory* translated by Dorothy L. Sayers. Reprinted by permission of Penguin Books Ltd; Thomas Wilson (1982) *Arte of Rhetoric* edited by Thomas J. Derrick. Reprinted by permission of Garland; Aristotle (1980) *The Nicomachean Ethics* translated by David Ross. Reprinted by permission of Oxford University Press; Terry Eagleton (1983) *Literary Theory: An Introduction*. Reprinted by permission of Blackwell Ltd; Gillian Beer (1970) *The Romance*. Reprinted by permission of Methuen and Co. Ltd.

1. Beginnings

'In the middle of the journey of this life of ours, I found myself in a dark wood where the straight path was lost...'
                                                        (Dante, *Inferno*, canto i)

There are ways in which this *Guide* will not interpret Spenser's poem for you. For a start, it is almost exclusively concerned with only the first three books of the *Faerie Queene*, the books constituting the poem's first published version in 1590. Neither will it give you finished and fully-developed readings of the allegory of any of the poem's first three books. Indeed, I claim in Chapter 3 that Spenser's allegorical poem demands the active engagement of its reader to produce allegory. Neither do I want in this *Guide* to prescribe certain sorts of interpretation. It is likely that sections of Spenser's poem contain topical and political allegories: this is thought especially true of Book V. But there seem to me to be few more daunting experiences for new (or for that matter old) readers of the *Faerie Queene* than to be told that a certain giant 'is' Philip II of Spain, an enchantress Mary Queen of Scots, and a particular incident represents Elizabeth's rejection of one of her suitors. I can remember that as a student I set out on the narrative quest of Book I armed with a postcard on which I had written the set of equations beginning 'Archimago = the Pope. Sir Satyrane = Sir John Perrot, the natural son of Henry VIII...', which you can find (but should not look at) in a footnote in the standard edition of Spenser's *Works*. This postcard proved to be an uninformative and distracting guide, one of the reasons why I did not reach the end of the *Faerie Queene* until many years later. Having now read Spenser's poem more often, I can see something of what the first equation was getting at, although I now find its curt equivalence is misleading and restricted: I still know nothing about Sir John Perrot.

I think that there are also disadvantages in offering finished and fully coherent theological, moral or other sorts of reading of any of the books for reasons I hope will emerge in the course of your reading of this *Guide*. Both Spenser's poem and its interpretation are, to borrow the title of a recent study of Book IV which itself borrows a Spenserian phrase, an 'endlesse worke' (IV xii 1.1).[1] The work of allegory points to the full presence of truth but can never provide it, or, to quote one of the poem's best and most practised readers, 'No genuine response to the poem is ever entirely wrong, only incomplete'.[2]

As the *Faerie Queene* is famous, even in the seventeenth century some would have said notorious, as an extended allegorical poem ('Allegories so wild, unnatural, and extravagant, as greatly displease the Reader'[3]), this *Guide* will in each chapter encourage you to think about the process of reading, and particularly of reading allegory. Allegory both is and is not a 'natural' way of reading. The *Faerie Queene* is a demanding poem and its demands are not just those of a difficult Renaissance play like *King Lear* or *Hamlet*. It requires not only an actively engaged reader, but a reader prepared to learn different sorts of reading. You will find passages of exposition in some chapters in the hope that they might provide guides in reading Spenser's poem. As cultural and theoretical contexts I have included passages from Spenser's predecessors and contemporaries,[4] such as those which discuss allegory and other issues in critical theory, passages about interpretation of texts, and passages from other sorts of Renaissance writing which I hope will provide relevant and illuminating comparisons. There are also some translations from writings in classical antiquity, for of course the Renaissance inherited, rediscovered, translated, revivified, imitated and thoroughly absorbed these texts. Although it is probably an illusion to think that we can respond in the same way to these different texts as Renaissance readers, my intention is to let you have access to ideas, theories and discussions which the writer of the *Faerie Queene* knew or could have known.

The way that the *Faerie Queene* encourages its reader to read is very much in the spirit of the series of which this book is part.

Let us start straight away at the very beginning of the *Faerie Queene* by looking at its first incident. The first six stanzas of I i give us portraits of an unnamed knight and lady. Then a storm arises in i 6 and the travellers take refuge in 'a shadie groue'. **Please read I i 1–27. Look up any words that are unknown, difficult or whose meanings you feel elude you. The notes at the end of Roche's Penguin edition gloss some difficult or archaic** words, but a good dictionary will give a greater variety of the senses of a word. In your experience of reading this passage do you have any difficulties in following or understanding what's happening? What is your position as reader in relation to the knight, the lady and the monster which is named at i 18.9? Is *your* reaction and perception the same as *theirs*? Please now re-read the *Faerie Queene* I i 1–27 and then make notes on these questions.

DISCUSSION

At first we and the travellers are 'Led with delight' (i 10.1), the wooded grove having offered pleasant refuge and the sweetness of birdsong, and the catalogued variety of trees (i 8–9) having provided leisurely scenic distraction for the poem's travellers and its readers. We 'beguile' ('wile away pleasantly') the way, but 'beguile' becomes more ominous ('cheat') as our relaxed wandering turns into losing our way. Stanzas 10–11 describe the travellers' confusion in the wood, but also surely are responsible for and describe our confusion as readers as we pick our way through the wandering syntax and uncertain sense of direction of these two stanzas. The syntax of i 10 wanders through the stanza as the paths and turnings of the wood are imitated in a loose succession of clauses introduced by relative pronouns ('When ... whence ... which ... when ...') whose referents we are unsure of. Confusion is increased in lines like 'Furthest from end then, when they neerest weene' (i 10.6). Which end? Nearest to what? Our confusion and uncertainty as readers, which are produced by the poetry's techniques, put us in the same 'diuerse doubt' as the characters whose wanderings the poem is telling us of. Having shared their delight we now share their doubt.

The beginning of i 11 promises resolution and its middle provides a sense of arrival. The knight and lady find a cave in the middle of the wood, now described as a 'labyrinth' (11.4), as we as readers find it in the middle of this stanza. In our reading we have enacted the wanderings and arrival of the travellers, but what this arrival and cave signify is in doubt. Finding the centre of a maze might mean arrival, solving a puzzle, finding a solution: alternatively something nasty might be lurking there, just as the Minotaur was at the centre of the labyrinth in Crete, or as monsters in films habitually lie in wait for us at the end of a series of winding passages. The lady is cautious. She voices our nervous reservations in a familiar proverb about hidden danger (12.4). As we have shared the wanderings of the poem's personages, so they are doing the same thing as us in their attempts to 'read' the wood, its turnings and possible significances. And by the end of i 13 we are aware of different perspectives on our recent communal experience, an experience and a wood which we now have named as 'wandring' (i 13.6). The knight is undaunted, but perhaps hasty and rash in his response, or at least so the lady thinks (11.7–12). She names the wood and warns that indeed a monster does lurk there (12–13). The Dwarf is terrified, understandably so after the lady's warning. We now have our own experience of the wood, mediated partly by the travellers' experience, the reactions so far of the figures in the poem to it, our sense of their various reactions and also a sense of what those reactions can tell us of levels of awareness represented in those figures. We have registered the loss of the way in the wood, but also the knight's rash eagerness, the lady's steady and well-informed caution: we have both a reading experience and the responses to a reading of the wood by fictional characters.

The knight, we presume from his description and behaviour, is a knight errant (an itinerant knight) and, at the risk of implying a typically Renaissance false etymology for the word, a knight charged with an errand (commission), to conquer a dragon (i 3). We and he have been errant in our wanderings in the wood: we have wandered and erred. And in the middle of this wood we discover (i 14ff) the monster Error, the personification of the bad meanings of erring and being errant.

Spenser is always playing on the different meanings of words and of names, and he revives old words and invents new ones. Ideally we should all use a good dictionary to investigate Spenser's use of words, especially when we suspect that a word (like 'error') is particularly significant. Such use of a dictionary will reveal the roots of words, their history and some of the range of meanings with which Spenser is constantly playing. Ideal for such an investigation is the new second edition of the big *Oxford English Dictionary* (20 vols, 1989); failing that, the two-volume *Shorter Oxford English Dictionary* (revised 3rd edition, 1973) is useful. If you look up 'error', 'errant' – and 'errand' – in a large dictionary you will find that the range of meanings of 'error', which comes ultimately from the Latin *errare*, 'to wander', is like the range of experiences between entering the wood and the defeat of the monster: travelling, roaming, wandering, winding course, erring in opinion, mistaking, transgressing. The initial delightful wanderings have become monstrous: Error's name is the name of the various experiences in the poem so far.

By the time we reach, with some relief, the completion of the episode and the lady's rejoicing at Error's defeat in i 27, I think no readers inside or outside the poem who have experienced Error are in any doubt about her disgusting unpleasantness. Error is ugly, dirty, poisonous, noisy. Her shape and size are nightmarish. Her evoked physicality is disgusting; she suckles her young from poisonous breasts (15.4–7), she vomits up her stinking half-digested food (20).

Why, do you think, is Error presented as she is, and with the characteristics she has? You could start, if you wish, by cataloguing her features and behaviour, then look for any organizing principles you can detect as determining those features. What features or motifs can you detect in her shape, behaviour and actions? Can you then relate them to any ideas you may now be forming about the concept of 'error'?

DISCUSSION

Here is my list of characteristics: monstrous, serpentine, half-human and hybrid, light-hating, prolific breeder, poisonous, unpleasant digestion. Some patterns gradually emerge: Error lives in a dark cave, she and her brood hate light, and the frogs and toads in her vomit lack eyes; feeding and digestion in this passage are disgusting and bizarre.

As we have seen, and experienced in our reading of Error, her actions are imaginatively disgusting to sight, hearing, touch, taste and smell. The poem wants us to find Error and error repulsive and nauseating. Error arouses a general disgust, but it is particularly the bodily functions of herself and her brood which offend our usual ideas of generation and feeding. And, I think, in both the shape of Error, and in the activities of herself and her brood, we can see embodied that primary reading experience of the poem's first incident: wandering, 'erring', a movement of confused recirculation. Error's shape, like the paths in the wood, is 'erring', twisted and contorted, labyrinthine, coiling and uncoiling (15–16): it is by wrapping the knight in her coils that she temporarily immobilizes and threatens to strangle him (18). So too her brood circulate oddly into, out of and in relation to her body: sucking her poisonous breasts (15.4–7), creeping suddenly back into her mouth in fear (15), being aggressively excreted, or expelled from her womb (22), and, having failed to gain re-entry at her mouth, sucking at her wound (25). Her feeding and digestion are imperfect and circular: she gulps in lumps and gobbets and vomits them out again. The representation of Error is partly determined by a knot of ideas about error as transgressive wandering.

Let us now try and look at the sort of writing employed in this passage. We and the knight have shared an experience: he struggled with Error, and in a sense we, through imaginative participation, might say the same, by using *figurative* language (the use of words with senses other than their literal or standard ones) about our reading experience of that participation. But, of course, we are simultaneously aware of reading a poem and a narrative and so can also talk more objectively of the knight's struggle with a personification of error. We share imaginatively in his struggle, even as we share in his nauseated disgust, but as readers we can also stand back and view it in a way that he cannot. For the figure of this knight, in a poetic fiction, the distinction between literal and figurative in this incident is not possible. For us awareness of this distinction is ultimately inevitable, essential to and caused by our reading of this poem. But the distinction can be blurred, as it is in the second sentence of this paragraph when I claim that we, too, might say we have struggled with error. Is there a difference between struggling with error and struggling with Error? I think that in talking critically about this incident we have to use a language which is poised between the literal and the figurative. **As an experiment, try and describe in short sentences, some literal and some figurative, characteristics of Error and her brood and their effects on the knight.**

DISCUSSION

I came up with, in no particular order: Error is disabling (18), Error loves obscurity (15–16), Error feeds on scraps and spews out foulness (20), feeding on dead error is self-destructive (25–26), Error is the mother of a vast number of monstrosities (15), to defeat error requires faith as well as strength (19–27), Error's products are a nuisance (22).

Even in attempts to use non-figurative language it is difficult to avoid the figurative. As Aristotle observed in the fourth century BC, everyone uses metaphors even in ordinary conversation.[5] I'm pretty sure that 'Error loves obscurity' is figurative, and almost sure that 'Error's products are a nuisance' and 'Error is disabling' are literal statements, but cannot be sure that the figurative is not present in all these sentences. And 'feeding on dead error is self-destructive' surely becomes more (more visibly?) figurative simply by changing it to 'feeding on dead Error . . .'. Attempts to describe in literal language an abstraction like error tend to blur into figures of speech.

We can see that the incidents in this short narrative episode are centrally determined by notions of error as wandering and making a mistake, and we can account for some other features of the monster and the narrative as imaginative renderings of ideas which add other characteristics to a concept of error: error loves obscurity, error only partially processes partial information and gives it out again in grotesque forms, error can be fatal (remember the clichés 'fatal mistake' and 'fatal error'). All these statements in the previous sentence are a sort of half-translation of moments in i 10–27. We read the writing in these stanzas as developing figurative statements, but the images and narrative also seem to arise with some ease and naturalness from ideas we might have about error, and they also arise from our imaginative participation in the poem and its experiences so far.

I seemed to be suggesting at times in the last paragraph that our reading of the writing in the poem so far was a natural activity: the poetic images and the narrative intensifying the sort of 'literal' statement we might make about error. Aristotle's observation, which I mentioned above, would also seem to imply the natural-ness of metaphor in ordinary discourse. The poem brings us to Error by having us and the knight, apparently in the normal course of things, first 'err' in reading. But we have also been simultaneously aware of the unnaturalness of our experiences in that we have a sense of distance as readers from these fictional figures and incidents (see p. 6), and your recent thinking about figurative language (pp. 6–7) has perhaps made you aware of issues of 'naturalness' and 'artifice' in language, even if the very fact that I have put these words in inverted commas is an admission that the distinction is problematic. If the poem in various ways is intent on involving us in its images and narrative by mediating to us the experiences of its characters, arousing strong reactions in the reader, causing pleasure, anxiety and disgust, it also simultaneously reminds us that its discourse, images and narrative are not natu-ralistic but are part of an elaborate poetic fiction and suggests that that fiction has some sort of symbolic content.

In this episode, in what ways do you think we are aware of and reminded that we are reading a poem? How prosaic or 'poetic' is the language generally? Are there some stanzas which are more obviously 'poetic' than others? What clues are there that might make us think that that this episode has significance other than simply telling the story of a knight's defeat of a monster?

DISCUSSION

I expect that you must be already aware in some ways of the activity of reading the *Faerie Queene* as a Renaissance poem because of the highly 'poetic' nature of Spenser's work. The verse form of this poem, the Spenserian stanza of eight iambic pentameters and a final hexameter which rhyme ABABBCBCC, was invented by Spenser and is obviously elaborately artificial and patterned especially in its interweaving rhymes. Spenser's language in this poem and in his earlier poem, *The Shepheardes Calender* (1st edition 1579), which often causes us to have recourse to a dictionary or glossary, is distinctly unnatural. We register it as distancing and deliberately antique, as did Spenser's contemporaries. Spenser's poetic language received some criticism in his own time. Ben Jonson said that Spenser 'in affecting the ancients, writ no language', and Sir Philip Sidney, although allowing that *The Shepheardes Calender* had much poetry in it, did not approve of the 'framing of his style to an old rustic language'.[6] Both Ben Jonson and Sidney register the distancing effect of Spenser's archaisms of language which work, as a fine phrase in the epistle to *The Shepheardes Calender* puts it, to represent 'an eternall image of antiquitie'.[7]

In addition, at the height of the knight's struggles there are two flagrantly poetic interventions in two *epic similes* (extended and elaborate similes, first used in Greek and Roman epic poems, which digress temporarily from the action in hand). **Where are these similes, and why do you think Spenser introduces them?** One is the inundation of the Nile (21) with its exotic geography and curious natural history, and the other a pastoral scene (23) which mixes the delights of an evening landscape with the humorous picture of the shepherd pestered by gnats. They snatch us momentarily away from our disgust at Error's vomit and her crawling brood, while at the same time forming an analogy with what is happening in the narrative. We register the poetic device which suddenly removes us from the poem's action and also recognize the figure of the epic simile by its characteristic self-introductions: 'As when . . . As . . .'. The difference in tone, the abrupt change of imagined location, and our awareness of the epic simile as a *trope* (traditional figure of speech) are uses of language and poetic effects that draw attention to themselves. We cannot help but be aware of their effect on us and so we become aware of our activity in reading the poem.

And unlike the travellers the monster does not remain unnamed, but the name given is not a particular proper-noun name such as Echidna or Melusine (names of similar shaped monsters from classical myth and fairy-tale, respectively). Instead it is the name of an abstraction, Error. We have already seen how the literal tends to blur into the figurative when we use language about abstractions, so this naming necessarily prompts us to expect that the literal fiction of the narrative might shade into significances other than a knight's struggle with a monster in a wood. Indeed at one point the speaking voice of the poem itself intervenes in an exclamation, 'God helpe the man so wrapt in *Errours* endlesse traine' (18.9), which looks both inward with agitated concern to the knight's particular and urgent predicament (caught in the toils of Error) and aphoristically outward to a predicament such as we all might face at any time in life, caught in the toils of error. This *sententia* (pithy saying, maxim) of the poet's draws attention to itself even in an episode where the characters themselves are prone to such aphorisms (cf. the knight's at 12.9, the lady's at 12.4 and 13.4–5). And finally we cannot help but be struck by the contents of Error's vomit, 'full of bookes and papers' (20.6). **Why do you think that these are particularized?**

DISCUSSION

Metaphors of eating and digestion often seem to be unobtrusively naturalized, even as Aristotle observed, in the way we talk of studying and reading in ordinary conversation: 'taking in information', 'devouring a book'. Ben Jonson's opinion that 'there be some men are born only to suck out the poison of books' offers an interesting way of looking at some of the imagery of the Error episode. One of the best-known quotations from Francis Bacon's essay 'Of Studies' elaborates the metaphor at the end of a passage on the proper use of reading,

> Read not to contradict and confute; nor to believe and take for granted; not to find talk and discourse; but to weigh and consider. Some books are to be tasted, others to be swallowed, and some few to be chewed and digested.[8]

If part of the way that Error is depicted is determined by the articulation of an idea about reading itself, there may also be a pun earlier in the lady's warning about the wood, 'I read beware' (13.8). One meaning is produced by a gloss of Spenser's 'read' as an archaism (an alternative spelling of 'rede' = 'advise') and is 'I advise caution', but if we take 'read' at its face value for a modern reader then the lady, very much in keeping with our sense of her

as cautious and better informed than any of us, is saying, 'My
interpretation [I read] of this wood is "Be cautious"'.

At this point you may be interested to discover what some other
readers have had to say about the episode with Error and to
compare your reading of the monster with theirs. The note at the
end of this paragraph will point you to references to a selection of
criticism in books and periodicals, roughly arranged in order of
length (and roughly in order of increasing abstruseness), which,
however, you should read only after you have finished working
through this book. You will find that they extend and contextualize
some of your own reading of this episode. Take from them what
you find useful in extending the reading you have already produced. You will probably also find that the critics make two sorts
of reference to material that is unfamiliar to you. The first is to
references and contexts (literary, cultural, mythological and so on)
that are likely to be strange to you. The second sort will relate this
episode to larger and subtly complex readings and interpretations
of *Faerie Queene*, Book I, and sometimes other books of the
poem. You might find your own unfamiliarity with these two
kinds of reference daunting and cry with the Dwarf, 'Fly fly . . .
this is no place for liuing men'. This being the case, I think that
it is better that initially you continue reading the poem independently and in dialogue with this *Guide*. Indeed, since the
poem's 'end' (intention) as expressed in the letter to Sir Walter
Ralegh (on page 15 of the Penguin edition), is 'to fashion a
gentleman or noble person in vertuous and gentle discipline', it is
a good idea for the moment to trust the poem, together with your
increasing and cumulative experience of it, to suggest ways of
reading and interpreting itself. On the other hand I would be
erring if I pretended that the *Faerie Queene* is not a difficult poem,
decorated with images, allusions and references that none of us
have at our fingertips, and that it is written within traditions of
literature, thought, imagery, ideology, theology and politics that
may now strike us as alien. The scholarship and criticism on
Spenser's poem that was already being produced in the seventeenth
century and has continued ever since now amounts, to borrow a
phrase from later in *Faerie Queene*, Book I, to 'a goodly heape'
(I iv 5.1). It is a tribute to the constant interest of readers in
the poem over four centuries, but it can also intimidate by its
vast accreted tradition of scholarship. The very size of some of
the living monuments to Spenser produced in this century – for
example, the Variorum edition of Spenser (1932–57, 11 vols,),
A. C. Hamilton's edition of the poem (1977, pp. xiii and 753),

and most recently *The Spenser Encyclopaedia* (1990, pp. 858) – can be off-putting: at once inspiring in that there is so much to say about Spenser, and dispiriting in that one cannot ever hope to master all that information. So if you do decide to pursue Error through the pages of some of these critics, do not feel that they are writing about things you ought to know about *now*. 'Of making books there is no end'[9]: so too the activities of reading and interpretation are endless ('God helpe the man so wrapt in *Errours* endlesse traine'). I think that it is better to come back later and build on your own experience of this episode by reading the comments of other readers and gradually assimilating the information they provide when you feel more at home with reading Spenser's poem and have read more of its narrative.[10]

When you do read these critics you will find a multiplicity of interpretations which read this episode in a variety of contexts. But we at the very beginning of the poem are most concerned with coming to grips with a short narrative and an arresting image which in a way stands like a preliminary illustrated frontispiece often found in Renaissance books, a picture whose curious and intriguing visual language necessarily involves us and engages us in acts of interpretation. This episode with Error may eventually unfold many successive significations, yet an encounter with error has particular and acute relevance at this moment to the activity of reading. Perhaps its most urgent significance, for both the knight at the outset of his adventures and for us at the beginning of our reading of a poem whose first book is largely concerned with that knight's adventures, is about reading and about interpretation itself, their pleasures and their perils.

2. Reading and Allegory

'O, there's nothing to be hoped for from her! She's as headstrong as
an allegory on the banks of Nile.'

(Sheridan, *The Rivals*, III iii)

Sheridan's Mrs Malaprop sometimes speaks wiser than she
knows. Her confusion of 'allegory' with 'alligator' captures for us
a history of deep critical fear and suspicion of that exotic and
voracious monster 'allegory', and in particular the dangerous
Spenserian sub-species. We have just tackled an analogous
Spenserian monster in Chapter 1. This second chapter will invite
you to do two things. First, we will engage in the exercise of
reading very closely the portraits of the knight and lady at the very
beginning of Spenser's poem, before they encounter Error. We
have already noticed the rudiments of allegory and allegorical
reading in discussing Error: we will now pursue that approach
more closely. Then, we will look at some ways in which we might
think of allegory.

Read all of *Faerie Queene*, I i, to get a general sense of the poem
and its opening narrative. Then read I i 1–2 very closely and look
up unfamiliar words, or words which you suspect are used in
unfamiliar ways (such as 'pricking', 'dints', 'fielde' in 1.1–4).
Read these stanzas closely, asking the following questions: What
can we say about the knight whose picture opens this poem? What
sense do we get of him? How? On the basis of what kind of
information (appearance, demeanour, weapons)? How do we read
the picture which the opening of this poem makes us envisage?
What (and how much or how little) does this poem choose to tell

us about the knight? How certain are we about the accuracy of our impressions? And, finally, what acts of interpretation do these two stanzas involve us in? Remember the way in the Error episode we both experienced the fiction and were simultaneously aware of our activity in reading.

DISCUSSION

Canto i opens with an unnamed knight riding across a plain. The imperfect tense 'was pricking' captures a motion that is continuing. The effect, a static picture which simultaneously evokes movement, is like a still from a film or, perhaps better, a freeze-frame being released again into a running film. I am struck by archaisms of language and spelling ('was pricking' for 'spurring on a horse'; and, most strikingly, the past participle 'Y cladd' for 'clothed' in 1.2), which cause a sensation of observing the past. Both we and Spenser's original readers, for whom many of these uses of language were also archaic, sense the antique (cf. Chapter 1, p. 8). My experience of reading through the stanza is like looking at a picture or some cartoons where an outline is gradually filled in, of deciphering a figure about which suggestions accumulate. The first line describes the knight merely as 'gentle'. This is the only qualification of the knight the first stanza positively commits itself to: 1.8 tells us only that the knight *seemed* 'iolly'. 'Gentle' probably suggests mildness of disposition to us. Its other, older meanings, residual now in 'gentleman', suggest, among many other things, excellence, nobility and rank. A gentleman was one who could bear arms, the very arms displayed in 1.2–5. Yet, do we not feel a tension between the gentle knight and the urgency or even discomfort of movement in 'pricking'? His location is similarly unspecified, and as undifferentiated as one could imagine. A plain is just that: plain, level, flat, open, unmarked. The noun has the same quality as some of the meanings of the adjective 'plain': looking at the dictionary, I see that the adjective 'plain' can mean clear, open, obvious, simple, without embellishment. As yet both knight and location share an unspecified, unmarked, simple blankness, yet the urgency of pricking is particular and disturbing. The rest of the stanza offers a possible interpretation of this figure of a knight by adding details which we as readers endow with significance. The simplicity continues in a child's picture of a knight: he has armour and weapons (of course the shield is silver, the adjective signifying both the metal and the colour – in heraldry they are the same), and the obligatory horse. I think that as readers we may even have a sense of cooperation in filling in the details ourselves, like colouring in a child's colouring-book.

The details describe the knight's outside and we infer the inner man from the external armour. Lines 3–4 of the first stanza invite us to interpret some signs on the armour. The marks on the armour are dents and scratches caused by many bloody battles. They are material marks, in that fighting has scratched the armour, and they are symbolic marks, tokens of past battles. We read in the marks the signs of past fighting, the knight's past battles. Line 5, the middle line and turning point of the Spenserian nine-line stanza, with its initial 'yet', disturbs the consistency of the picture we (I, you and the text) have been collusively reading and constructing. *This* knight, apparently, has never managed weapons before. We have assumed the arms are his personal property, and inferred his past fights from the marks on them. We have made assumptions about the knight on the strength of signs provided by the armour in which he is covered. The paradox of a knight dressed in dented armour, but who has never until now carried arms, introduces a doubt, an ambiguity and uncertainty about the knight, the text and our reading of it. The text commits itself to the dints as true signs of many battles, a truthful relation of sign to meaning (1.4), but not to the dented armour as a necessarily truthful sign of this particular knight's experience or identity. We, cooperating with possibilities in the text, might have inferred wrongly about the knight. We have inferred experience (and presumably success) on the strength of our assumption that the armour is exclusively his. How we might apportion responsibility between ourselves, the text, and our cooperation for this wrong reading strikes me as an interesting question. Whose fault was it? Do we *necessarily* jump to the wrong conclusion? Is it the text's arrangement and ordering of signs that actually misguides us? How far can we trust verbal and pictorial signs? Can they, will they, ever speak unambiguously? This very paragraph, in the second chapter of this *Guide* to the *Faerie Queene*, repeats the (deceitful?) ambiguity above in the apposition, 'signs of past fighting, the knight's past battles', allowing (inviting?) the identification of the two parts of the apposition. How responsible is *my* text here of further misleading its readers on exactly the same point?

The reading of the significance of the knight's relationship to his arms, those material objects and also signs ('arms' means defensive armour, offensive weapons and also heraldic insignia on a shield) which we expect to constitute his identity, is apparently problematic. His surroundings are blank (plain) and currently offer no information. The other relationship in stanza 1 is, of course, that of the knight to his horse: from ancient times the possession of a steed constituted a man as a knight, as we can see in classical Rome in the relationship of *eques* (knight) to *equus* (horse), and in the German *Ritter*, rider, hence knight. After the central unsettling paradox in 1.5 the rest of the first stanza is taken up with the knight and his horse, even as the first half was taken up with the knight and his arms. The second half implies relationships between horse and rider, relationships which respond to the pricking which opened the stanza. The word 'angry' (1.6) could simply indicate that the horse is physically inflamed and smarting from being spurred, but we are likely to read the adjective as 'wrathful', which seems confirmed by 'chide' later in the same line. Our reading of the horse's reactions personify it. Animals may be actively angry (or is this, too, a human projection of our feelings on to them?), but they certainly cannot verbally chide (complain, rebuke). The text subtly offers us the horse in human terms, it invites us to think of it metaphorically. Line 6 moves from the ambiguity of 'angry' as either passively, physically smarting from spur and bit, or 'enraged', to a horse humanly scolding in 'chide'. The blurring of the distinction between animal and human here is continued in the uncertainty of the antecedent for the possessive in 'his foming bitt'. The bit is 'his' in that it is the possession of the knight who controls the horse with it, but also 'his' in that it is part of the tack of the *horse*, which is controlled by it. Since the distinction between animal and human is blurred, we may reflect not only on the way that the horse is made human, but also conversely on the relationship of the knight to the temper of his horse, that is, to see the horse's mettlesomeness as an indicator of its rider. So, can we not think of the horse and its behaviour as being a sort of figure for the nature of the knight? The blurrings between knight and horse are rather like the regular uncertainties we have about whether language is figurative or literal (see Chapter 1, p. 6).

Line 7 glosses 'did chide': 'As much disdayning to the curbe to yield'. 'As' either offers a possible explanation (the horse chided *because* it was angrily indignant about the bridle) or introduces a similitude (*like* one who scornfully thinks the bridle beneath him), thus repeating and admitting to the metaphorization in the previous line. The one noun in 1.7, 'curbe', is at once both literal (a strap under the jaw of a horse) and metaphorically figurative (restraint). The stanza's last two lines briefly rehearse its twofold problem of interpretation: the ambiguous relationship of sign to truth and the slippery relationship of literal and figurative in metaphor, familiar to us from Chapter 1 and rehearsed again by this stanza. Line 8 again suggests a visual appearance of the knight ('iolly', 'faire'), but both descriptions are severely qualified: the knight only *seemed* jolly. The adjective itself can have many meanings: in the dictionary in front of me, cheerful, handsome, exhilarated, over-confident, amorous and lustful are only some of them. The word 'faire' repeats the ambiguity of 'seemd' in its power to evoke both appearance and reality and allow the possibility of a discrepancy, well-known to the Witches in *Macbeth*, between them. Ambiguities multiply at the end of the line as the innocent 'sitt' might also mean 'well suited'. The last line of the stanza begins with the same evasive introductory 'as' as 1.7, so it actually declares that the knight is *like* a man with the necessary qualifications for jousts and battles. Strangely, this knight can be metaphorically like an able knight. The elusiveness of metaphor is redoubled by the ambivalence of 'fitt': he is well suited, qualified to be a knight, or only well rigged out as one, the furnishings not necessarily making, or bearing truthful witness to, the man.

The second stanza offers another expected, informing and constitutive relationship, the crucial relationship of the knight to his lord. It offers another inscribed sign ('badge . . . was also scor'd'), as the knight is marked twice, on breast and shield, with the lord's cross. As in i 1 the knight's identity remains problematic because of ambiguity and paradox. Lines 1 and 8 open with 'But', and line 9 with 'Yet'. The unnamed lord himself is also paradoxical: 'dying' (not dead) in 2.2, yet adored by the knight cryptically as 'And dead as liuing euer' (2.4). Part of the ambiguity is caused by the superscription of lord on knight. Just as the lord's cross (the cross was the mark used instead of a signature by many people, especially the illiterate, in documents) is inscribed on the knight's breast and shield, so the dense confusion of eleven male pronouns (he, him, his) in this stanza blurs a sharp distinction between knight and lord (who is 'he' in 2.7?). The stanza makes possible, but by no means certain, the identification of knight with lord. We may reasonably infer that a knight marked twice with a cross is likely in some way to have Christ as the paradoxical lord alluded to. The bloody cross will also in fact be revealed as the sign of the knight's name, which is finally given in the narrative at I ii 15.1. Naming of characters is regularly delayed in the poem while we read pictures and signs, and produce a meaning which is then named by the text, as we saw in the encounter with Error. Given this process of interpretation and then naming, it must be with deliberate irony that the first character to be named in the poem is identified by her name as 'mistake' (I i 13.6).

These stanzas engage us in 'reading' the knight and also often have us consider *how* we read and interpret, how accurately and with what degree of certainty. The final impressions of this knight at the end of stanza 2 remain ambiguous and paradoxical. The last two lines balance introductory 'but' against 'yet', and tell us that a knight who seemed jolly previously in 1.8 now seems 'too solemne sad', and in a final antithesis that he is feared, not fearful. He is apparently still in the process of definition, still a field for inscription. The sign inscribed upon him, the simple and positive mark of the cross, seems clearer and more certain than the field of its inscription. (In the sixteenth century it actually began the alphabet on a child's slate.) With numerous signs, badges and writings in these first two stanzas, we can even reflect that the poem itself opens with acknowledgement of its own inscribing. Since among the older meanings of 'pricking' is marking paper with pricks or dots, writing down, the poem punningly opens with its own inscription on the blank ('pricking on the plain').

Now carefully read the description of the lady in i 4–5, asking the same questions (What is she like? How do we know?) and using the same techniques that have begun to emerge in your reading of the knight. Do you detect any similarities, parallels, differences, symmetries in the two descriptions? Are they dressed or mounted in the same ways? Are there any ways in which your reading of the knight helps your reading of the lady? Given our experience of the reading of signs with the knight, is this lady what she seems? Is she really fair? Does your reading of the lady in any ways retrospectively illuminate your reading of the knight?

DISCUSSION

I will be briefer about the lady. As we might expect, a lady rides beside this knight and, as we might expect, she is 'faire'. Given our experience of this word at 1.8, we may wonder at its significance. Is she really beautiful? (Isn't 'faire' tautologous after 'louely', or do you think that the text is insistently reiterating her beauty?) Is she simply gracefully good at riding ('faire' as an adverb modifying 'rode')? Is she fair in comparison with the knight ('him faire *beside*')? We saw the knight's significance in elements constituting his knighthood (arms, horse, lord). The word 'beside' puts the lady in relationship to him and presumably him in relationship to the lady. Knights and ladies, a formulaic couplet for the author of the Proem to the whole poem (Proem 1.5), constitute each other complementarily, both socially and erotically. The sense that knight and lady may each decipher the other is supported by the parallels between the two descriptions. Two stanzas concentrate on each figure. The first lines of stanzas 1 and 4 begin with the same grammatical structure: definite article + adjective + common noun + verb of motion. Both lines end by locating the respective figures: the knight in relation to the uncertain blank plain, the lady in relation to the knight. Both are mounted, but the lady on a quiet, humble ass which is the antithesis of the knight's mettlesome horse. If we found the knight constituted in relation to his horse and its qualities, then we may similarly transfer the ass's humility as a property of its rider. 'Yet' in 4.3 does not introduce a paradox to us, as it did in 1.5, but rather an attempt at clarification, a clarification of 'white' which is a synonym for the potentially dubious 'faire' of 4.1. The ass is white, even whiter than snow, yet the lady is whiter than the ass and so whiter than both ass and snow. The commonplace simile which this comparison elaborates is of course 'as white as snow', usually used with absolute implication, that is, we compare white things to snow, the whitest thing we can imagine. But here snow is the lowest term, with ass and lady in ascending order of intenser whiteness. The degrees are like those of adjectival positive (white/snow), comparative (whiter/ass) and superlative or absolute (whitest/the lady). So, in this series the lady herself becomes the absolute standard by which the other degrees of whiteness may be gauged. The knight's outside led to the reader's wrong inference about his history and what he might be. The lady's nature (she is whitest of all, whiter than her ass which is seen, and whiter than snow which is called in for comparison) is declared, and then we are told that it is hidden from both the world of the poem and us. The technique is the very opposite to that in depicting the knight. He was wrongly inferred on the strength of a external description. The lady is declared to be absolutely white although at this moment in the fiction of the poem such whiteness cannot be seen. We are asked at this point to trust the veracity of the text that the lady is superlatively beautiful. Yet the text hides that superlative whiteness under a veil and then a black stole, itself throws a veil over what it has declared to be true.

What I have been asking you to practise as readers of Spenser's poem and of this chapter, and what has been practised so far by myself and this book, is close reading, with particular attention to the many meanings of words. Although the *Faerie Queene* is a long poem it will respond, stanza by stanza, to the same detailed critical scrutiny we might be more inclined to apply to a short lyric. I am not suggesting that we are going to read the poem all the way through in this close, detailed way, but I am suggesting that if we had the time the poetry of the *Faerie Queene* would bear this sort of detailed investigation. We have also been practising formalist criticism, or 'New Criticism'. We have even perhaps been doing a simple form of structuralist criticism in that, in this small section of the poem, we have been intent on a set and system of words and signs and their relationships to each other, words whose meanings we try to interpret on the basis of the information and interrelationships the words themselves display in five stanzas of the poem. We have been examining the significance of the knight, and then the lady, in terms of some relationships offered internally in the portraits of each in the text, and then the portraits in relation to each other. We have been reading textually. One of the approaches of this *Guide* will be sometimes to pay this close attention to the text of the poem and to the internal interrelationships of words, signs and pictures, interrelationships which will necessarily define, redefine and complicate each other the more we read the poem.

I think that close reading is the most useful first step towards considering the poem as *allegory*, that is, the way the poem's fictions suggest to us, by resemblance, structured meanings which are not simply those of its narrative. 'What is chiefly needed to understand the allegory fully' writes A. C. Hamilton, 'is to understand all the words'.[1] This strikes me as both a daunting statement, for there is an enormous number of words in the *Faerie Queene* (I guess well over 300,000), and also a heartening one, for Hamilton encourages me to think that the best approach to Spenser's allegory is not primarily vast knowledge but attentive reading. But, to invoke Hamilton again: '*The Faerie Queene* accommodates many kinds of readers. No genuine response to the poem is ever entirely wrong, only incomplete'.[2] This *Guide*, too, will attempt to indicate the accommodation of many readings.

Let us now turn from the purely textual to the *intertextual*,[3] that is to say, the relation of texts to other texts and in this case the relationship of the five stanzas of our text to other texts. We found that the knight and lady set up a structure of internal significances partly because of the ways in which they resembled and differed from each other. 'Allegory', said one early authority, 'is talking about something else'.[4] If my provisional description of allegory in the previous paragraph is at all correct, that is, a suggestion by resemblance of structured meanings which are not simply those of its narrative, then allegory might establish significance partly by the way that texts relate to each other.

Let us look at an intertextual relationship between the description of the knight and a passage from the New Testament, from the Geneva Bible (1560)[5] version of part of Paul's letter to the Ephesians. As you will see, in the Geneva Bible the text comes with marginal glosses, which offer sixteenth-century interpretations of the passage's figurative language. **Please read the following extract (Ephesians 6:11–17) carefully:**

Put on the [1]whole armour of God, that ye may be able to stand against the assaults of the devill.

For wee wrestle not against [2]flesh and blood, but against principalities, against powers, and against the worldly governours, the princes of the darkenes of this worlde, against spirituall wickednesses, which are in the hie places.

For this cause take unto you the whole armour of God, that ye may be able to resist in the evil day, and having finished all things, stand fast.

Stand therefore, and your loynes girde about with veritie, and having on the brestplate of [3]righteousnesse.

And your feete shod with the [4]preparation of the Gospell of peace.

Above all, take the shield of faith, wherewith yee may quench all the fierie darts of the wicked.

And take the helmet [5]of salvation and the sword of the Spirite, which is the word of God.

[1] or, complete harnesse.

[2] The faithfull have not onely to strive against men and themselves, but against Satan the spirituall enemy, who is most dangerous: for he is over our heads, so that we cannot reach him, but he must be resisted by God's grace.

[3] Innocencie and godly life

[4] That ye may be readie to suffer al things for the Gospell
Isa 59.17
1 Thes 5.8

[5] The salvation purchased by Jesus Christ

Now consider first the passage's use of figurative language, remembering our consideration of Error. How does the passage use language whose meaning is not exclusively literal? How are the images (for example, shield, helmet) in the passage organized? What relationship might a reading of this passage have to a reading of the knight? How do the glosses affect either reading?

DISCUSSION

This text talks of a spiritual struggle and does so through a series of metaphors which express virtues and abstractions as pieces of armour. They are metaphors of the purest kind in that they express comparison very briefly without explicit acknowledgement of 'like' or 'as' simile does, and express identity rather than likeness: the breastplate *is* righteousness, rather than is *like* it, the shield is faith. The text focuses the reader's attention on the material objects; we imagine the various pieces of armour and almost see the implied soldier, like a diagram in a book, equipped with labelled weapons: a helmet called 'Salvation', a sword called 'Spirite'. In this series of metaphors we are given very concisely both images and the abstractions they signify, that is, we envisage image (shield), have named the virtue (faith), and are told that the shield means faith in the acknowledgement of the metaphor in 'of'. Metaphor asserts simultaneously the identity *and* difference of the two terms in its comparison. The Epistle to the Ephesians asserts metaphorically that a breastplate *is* righteousness, but only on the understanding that breastplate and righteousness are also two different things. The metaphors here are organized in that their economy is that of a soldier's panoply. They are in fact one simple form of allegory, the extension of a metaphor throughout a passage, or, as one Elizabethan literary theorist put it, repeating a long-standing rhetorical definition, 'a long and perpetuall Metaphore'.[6] This 'whole armour of God' passage is an example of allegory as trope (traditional figure of speech, see Chapter 1, p. 8) where allegory is a figure of speech which is an expanded and continued metaphor.

And if I apply my own provisional definition of allegory on p. 19 then I could say that this passage suggests by resemblance a structure of virtues and abstractions necessary for spiritual struggle, even as the whole panoply of armour is necessary for physical fighting.

The literal level of the allegory is the description of the arming of a soldier for physical fighting. The figurative level speaks of spiritual conflict, and the pieces of a soldier's equipment are virtues and abstractions needed for defence and offence. The glosses in the Geneva Bible offer further explication of this particular 'perpetuall Metaphore', such as particularizing 'righteousness' as 'innocencie and godly life'. It seems to me that this explication limits and restricts the figurative meanings possible. For example, I think 'the brestplate of righteousnesse' might mean all sorts of things which I might generally (and clumsily) sum up as 'the self-protection afforded by virtue': 'Innocencie and godly life' would not have been the first gloss I would have thought of. In the glosses' cross-references the Geneva Bible is producing its own intertextualities. The verse in Thessalonians describes the children of day having such armour, and Isaiah 59:17 describes God himself putting on similar armour to avenge himself against wickedness. Ephesians 6 obviously arms its spiritual warrior like

Isaiah's God: its allegory is analogous to an allegory in Isaiah, and indeed probably deliberately models itself on it. Here, then, in a self-conscious analogue, a New Testament allegory is modelled on an Old Testament allegory. The technical term for the persistent and widespread habit of interpretation in Western Christian culture which saw Old Testament passages anticipating or prefiguring those in the New Testament is *typology*.

I think that an awareness of the relationship between our reading of this passage from Ephesians and *Faerie Queene*, I i 1–2, supports, but by no means brings to closure, our interpretation of the opening of the poem. The armour is the property not just of this knight, but also of spiritual warriors in other texts. As one eighteenth-century commentator on the poem put it, 'this panoply has been worn by every Christian man in every age'.[7] This reader's interpretation is relevant to the Christian warrior of Ephesians, Spenser's knight and presumably himself. Constituents of a typical chivalric description are analogous, then, to images we find in a Scriptural text. As Ephesians 6 has a New Testament allegory analogous to an Old Testament one (Isaiah 59:17), so the opening of the *Faerie Queene* presents us with a chivalric allegory analogous to one in the New Testament. In Ephesians 6 it is fairly easy to see the way the figurative language carries the spiritual meaning, for the 'perpetuall Metaphore', the trope of allegory, of arming the spiritual warrior stands out from the rest of the chapter's discourse, which is taken up initially with exhortation and regulation of families and households and finally with a formal valediction. And in the Geneva Bible text the marginal glosses show the production of allegory in even sharper relief by extending and making visible acts of interpretation.

At the beginning of the *Faerie Queene* we have no surrounding non-figurative discourses or marginal glosses to focus our attention on figurative language. But, as we have seen, I i 1–5 insistently draw our attention to problems of appearance and reality, signs and what they might signify, identity and its outward manifestations, to likenesses of truth, and to metaphor. That is, the stanzas themselves draw the reader's attention to the problematic activities of sustained reading and interpretation of 'perpetuall Metaphore'. Like this particular *Guide* and the series of which it is part, the text of the *Faerie Queene* engages its reader in a dialogue about production of meaning proceeding from the cooperation of the reader with the text, or indeed from the reader's divergence from or resistance to it. We may also note that intertextuality is not just a matter of relationships between texts, but also of relationships between texts and the interpretations they have acquired in history. Spenser's picture of an armed knight might not only have a relation to the armed warrior of Ephesians 6, but also to interpretations of that figure. Spenser says as much himself in the letter to Ralegh; 'that is the armour of a Christian man specified by Saint Paul' (Penguin edition, p. 17). Not that we should assume, I think, that the Geneva gloss 'solves' questions of interpretation of Spenser's knight. After all, the Geneva gloss is commenting on Ephesians 6, and commenting in the sixteenth century on the Epistle to the Ephesians, not on Spenser. We are reading Spenser at the end of the twentieth century. Although we may now wish to consider and incorporate into our reading of Spenser added knowledge of a glossed scriptural text, I think that this should enlarge rather than limit our reading. We see *in addition* that the knight's battle is and has been the battle of the Christian man, that his defence is faith (his shield), and so on. Indeed, knowledge of the scriptural text enlarges an understanding of both Spenser and St Paul. It is only by thinking about and working on the relationship between allegories in these two pieces of text in Ephesians and *Faerie Queene*, I i 1–2 that I have realized and added to my sense of the opening of the *Faerie Queene*, the analogous intertextuality between Ephesians 6 and Isaiah. I suggested above that reducing figurative language to a literal paraphrase reduced our interpretative options. So allegory, which we have so far experienced largely as our 'perpetuall Metaphore', seems to me to delight in an expanding of meaning, rather than to seek its delimitation.

Now look at another instance of intertextuality in another passage from the Epistles (Geneva Bible, 2 Corinthians 3:13–17). Consider also this passage in relation to your reading experience of the lady in *Faerie Queene*, I i 4–6.

And wee are not as Moses, which [1]put a vaile upon his face, that the children of Israel should not looke unto the ende of that which should be abolished.

Therefore their mindes are hardened: for untill this day remayneth the same covering untaken away in the reading of the olde testament, which vaile in Christ is put away.

[1]Moses shewed the Law as it was covered with shadowes, so that the Jewes eyes were not lightened, but blinded, and so coulde not come to Christ, who was the ende thereof: againe the Gospel setteth foorth the glory of God cleerely, not

But even unto this day,
when Moses is read, the vaile
is laid over their hearts.
    Nevertheless, when
their heart shall be turned to
the Lorde, the vaile shall be
taken away.
    Now the [2]Lord is the
Spirit, and where the Spirit
of the Lord is, there is
liberty.
    But we all beholde as
in a [3]mirrour the glorie of the
Lorde with open face, and
are changed into the same
image, from glorie to glorie,
as by the Spirit of the Lord.

covering our eyes, but
driving the darkenesse
away from them.

[2] Christ is our
mediator, and authour
of the new Testament,
whose doctrine is
spiritual, and giveth
life to the
Law.
John 4.24

[3] In Christ, who is God
manifested in the flesh, we
see God the Father as in a
most cleare glasse.

You could read the whole chapter, and watch out for figurative
language and metaphors. What does the chapter have to say about
truth and its representation?

DISCUSSION

At the beginning of 2 Corinthians 3 the writer feels obliged to
commend his own sincerity, integrity and truth, and writes that
his addressees are evidence of his integrity as they are themselves
genuine inscriptions of truth (verses 1–4). A series of antitheses
are then constructed – old covenants, written law, stone inscriptions, letters, death and condemnation, against, respectively, a
new covenant, spirit, the human heart, spirit, life, acquittal – in
short, the antithesis is between restricted and restrictive texts, on
the one hand, and freedom of interpretation, on the other (verses
5–11). The relationship between these antitheses, between old
and new agreements and understandings, finds expression in a
new free exegesis of an old text, Exodus 34:29ff, the description
of Moses' descent from Mt Sinai, his face, subsequently veiled,
shining from recent nearness to the divine presence. The passage's
exegesis of this figure of a veiled Moses is complex. He is a figure
of the old restrictive dispensation, splendid yet limited, which
nevertheless proleptically gives hope for even greater splendour
under a new dispensation. The veil becomes a figure for the very
inability of Israelites of the Epistle's time to interpret the veil. That
is, some interpreters of the veil cannot see behind the veil to the
truth it veils, which is itself a prefiguration of a greater splendour
and liberty which has now arrived. The figure of the veil,[8] then, is

partly a figure about figurative language and its relation to truth eventually revealed. It is also a figure here for the interpretation of the Old Testament as prefiguring the New and so for inter-textuality between them. Paradoxically, then, the veiled Moses is (inadequately interpreted) a figure of blind, restricted and inade-quate interpretation, but at the same time (the spirit of its meaning properly interpreted) a figure of latent and splendid truth. In this passage, then, the figure of the veiled Moses can be the subject of many interpretations: the reflected but transient splendour of the Old Law, the relation of old and new dispensations, an inability properly to interpret, but also prefiguration of the new law, hence concealed truth. This one figure can apparently be *polysemous*, that is, it simultaneously offers many meanings.

Again, the application of this text to Spenser's figure of the veiled lady confirms and extends our exercise in close reading. Rightly understood, both the veiled Moses and the lady are figures of veiled truth. Both draw attention to concealment of splendour, and both require acts of reading faith in a truth which is asserted but hidden. Indeed, the figures of both the veiled Moses and Spenser's lady lead us to consider the relation of the figurative and fictional surfaces of texts to underlying truth ('when Moses is read the vaile is laid over their hearts'). With the assistance of the figure of the lady we may now wish to describe the knight in the light of our experience of reading her. The truth of her hidden inner beauty and integrity comments on his exterior show which mis-leadingly implies experience. The slow stability of her progress measures his barely curbed restiveness. Her consistent although cryptic truth deciphers more clearly his inconsistencies. Her veil is a conscious and truthful self-admission of concealment which contrasts with the unstated possibilities of ambiguity and deception represented in the knight's armour.

So far I have been trying to do several things in this chapter. The first is to encourage you in what is (I hope) a benevolent variety of critical practice of the Wackford Squeers school: finding out about allegorical reading by doing it ('We go upon the practical mode of teaching, Nickleby; the regular education system . . . When the boy knows this out of book, he goes and does it'). However we might theorize or define allegorical reading, or however we think of its history – and I shall glance at these areas in a moment – I am sure that Spenser's allegorical poem primarily demands our participation and cooperation in construct-ing allegory. Spenser's allegory is produced and discovered by doing it. This means that the focus of the practice of allegory is on the reader. Spenser's letter to Ralegh indicates that the poem's author encourages us to read in this way, for 'The generall end therefore of all the booke is to fashion a gentleman or noble person in vertuous and gentle discipline' (Penguin edition, p. 15). We readers must contribute to the construction of the poem's meaning, even though we immediately experience the mistakes and dangers of such contributory participation in early stanzas of the poem. Perhaps, inevitably, 'strict interpretation begins with misunderstanding'.[9]

If you wish to read a good brief piece about allegory in general, the article in *The Spenser Encyclopaedia* is excellent in its scope and subtlety, and the bibliography at its end will give you more than enough in the way of further reading about allegory.[10] For the time being, and in the light of what we have been looking at in this chapter, you might think of allegory in various ways.

1   Allegory as a practice of active reading we are already engaging in. In this way allegory may be seen as making great demands on its readers so that they may produce its meanings. Seen in this way, allegorical writing may be usefully thought of in terms of those twentieth-century critical theories which see the reader as the most important producer of meaning in a text, not the author. In the light of this chapter's stress on our active participation as readers and on the interrelated play of texts, you may find Roland Barthes' ideas about writing particularly applicable to allegory:

> a text is made of multiple writings, drawn from many cultures and entering into mutual relations of dialogue, parody, contestation, but there is one place where this multiplicity is focused and that place is the reader, not, as was hitherto said, the author.[11]

2   Allegory as a trope, that is, a figure of speech like metaphor and simile. We have seen an example of this in the Epistle to the Ephesians. The most obvious examples of allegory as trope are personified abstractions. Error has provided one sort of example of these. You could look at some Spenserian examples from later in the poem, some of which we will encounter in our reading, some not. Read in Book I, for example, the descriptions of any one or more of the Seven Deadly Sins (I iv 18ff) or of the virtues in the House of Celia (I x). Despair (I ix 28ff) is an extended example of the depiction of a personified abstraction. Try thinking about the ways in which the extended metaphor of the abstraction they represent is realized in the details of these figures' appearance, behaviour and actions. Again, you will find that the exercise of reading Error will provide a useful model. Elsewhere in the *Faerie Queene* you can find such obviously named personifications

as Lust (IV vii 5ff), Sclaunder (IV viii 23ff) and Envy (V xii 27ff), and personified abstractions whose names are derived from the qualities they represent: look, for example at Ignorance (Ignaro, I viii 30ff) and Charity (Charissa, I x 29ff). You will be able to find many more.

3 Allegory as an entire cast of mind was prevalent in western European culture up to and including the Renaissance, and also survived after it. This habit of thought assumed that not only literary texts, but also the created world itself, was a set of meaningful signs in which human readers might decipher messages about truth and about natural and metaphysical realities. The metaphors of the world as a book or a mirror were frequently used. The notion of the world as a book to be allegorically read and interpreted was common and durable: in the twelfth century the theologian and mystic, Hugh of St Victor, saw the earth 'like a book written by the finger of God' and in the seventeenth century the poet, Abraham Cowley, was still using the same metaphor in a poem on Dr William Harvey, who discovered the circulation of the blood:

> Thus Harvey sought for truth in truth's own Book,
> The creatures, which by God himself was writ

You will become familiar with this cast of mind the more you read of Spenser's poem.

I wrote earlier that allegory seemed to me to delight in a plenitude of meanings, and earlier still we saw that it was possible for the figure of the veiled Moses in 2 Corinthians to offer simultaneously many meanings. The thirteenth-century theologian Thomas Aquinas asks the question 'Can one passage of Scripture bear several senses?' when he is writing about allegory in Scripture, a topic we have already briefly considered in reading and interpreting some passages from Pauline Epistles. It is in the Epistles we can find the word 'allegory' uniquely used in the New Testament.[12] Aquinas raises the objection that many simultaneous and coexisting meanings to a passage of text would confuse and deceive. Yet there was a tradition, which we will notice at the end of this chapter, that there were at least four senses to Scripture. Aquinas solves his problem by arguing that words are signs of things and God has authored things (such as events, objects, even history) which themselves have further and other meanings. Human authors inscribe words which are signs for things. God also inscribes *things* having meaning, that is he also authors the material things to which words refer. Perhaps the contrast between part of the entry for 'lion' in the *Shorter Oxford English*

Dictionary and what a lion can mean for the writer of a medieval bestiary vividly illustrates this third sense of allegory as a cast of mind. The modern dictionary gives us:

> A large carnivorous quadruped, *Panthera leo*, now found native only in Africa and southern Asia, of a tawny colour, and having a tufted tail, and in the male . . . a flowing shaggy mane.

And here is an entry in an old bestiary:

The lion

So Jacob, blessing his son Judah, says 'Judah is a lion's whelp, the son from my seed. Who shall rouse him?' [Genesis 49.9]. The *Physiologus* says that the lion has three characteristics. The first is that it prowls in the mountains, and if it happens to be stalked by hunters it scents the hunter and, wherever it goes, completely covers over the tracks behind it with its tail so that the hunter, following its tracks, cannot find its lair and capture it.

Just so our Saviour, spritually the lion of Judah's tribe, the rod of Jesse, son of David [Revelation 5.5], sent from above from the Father, hid from discovery the tracks of his godhead . . . as he came down into a virgin's womb and saved mankind which had lost its way. As he ascended to his Father, angels on high ignorant of this said to those who were ascending with the Lord, 'Who is this King of glory' and they answered 'The Lord of hosts, he is the king of glory' [Psalms 24.10].

The second characteristic of the lion is that when it sleeps its eyes are watchful, they remain open. So in the Song of Songs the bridegroom says 'I am asleep, but my heart is awake' [Song of Songs 5.2]. So, while our Lord fell asleep in his human body on the cross and was buried, his godhead remained awake: 'Behold, he who watches over Israel neither slumbers nor sleeps' [Psalms 121.4].

The third characteristic is that when the lioness gives birth to the cub it is born dead and she watches over it for three days. The father comes on the third day, breathes in its face and revives it. Just so did the almighty Father raise from the dead his son, our Lord Jesus Christ on the third day, as Jacob says, 'He will fall asleep like a lion, and like a lion's cub. Who shall rouse him?' [Genesis 49.9].[13]

The modern dictionary definition limits and pinpoints meaning: the medieval bestiary definition encourages meaning to proliferate and spread.

I want to end this chapter by looking at a brief theoretical codification of allegory by Dante and also at an example of his own practice of allegory in an intertextually related moment in *Purgatory*, a section of his long allegorical poem, *The Divine Comedy*. This entails a temporary digression from Spenser's poem, but I think the two passages from Dante will allow you to see clearly some of the ideas that have arisen and that we have been considering in this chapter. They will also provide a useful opportunity for summary.

Some time after 1319 Dante wrote a letter to an Italian nobleman, Can Grande della Scala, addressing him as patron and friend. In it he dedicates to him *Paradise*, the last part of the *Divine Comedy*, and also alludes to the allegorical nature of his poem. In the following passage you will find some of the points already familiar: the polysemy of interpretation, intertextuality, the importance of the interpretation of the Bible, the way significances in Old Testament texts are seen as prefiguring those in the New.

> So, to clarify what we have to say: you should know that the meaning of this work is not simply a single one: on the contrary it may be termed 'polysemous', that is, having several meanings. One sense it has is through the letter, another is through the things signified by the letter. The first is called 'literal', the second the 'allegorical' or the 'mystical'. To make it plainer, this way of treating things can be examined in relation to these verses:
>
> When Israel came out of Egypt,
>   Jacob from a people of outlandish speech,
> Judah became his sanctuary,
>   Israel his dominion.
>
> [*In exitu Israel de Aegypto, domus Jacob de populo barbaro, facta est Judaea sanctificatio eius, Israel potestas eius*: Psalms 114:1–2]. If we look at just the literal sense, then the verse signifies to us the exodus of the children of Israel from Egypt in the time of Moses. If we look at the allegorical, then it signifies to us our redemption effected by Christ. If we look at the moral sense, it signifies to us the soul's turning away from sin's sorrows and wretchedness to a state of grace. The anagogical sense signified is the holy soul's release from the slavery of this corruption to the freedom of everlasting glory. And although these mystical senses are called by various names, generally one may term them all 'allegorical', as they are different from the literal or historical. For 'allegory' comes from the Greek *alleon* which is translated by the Latin 'other' [*alienum*] or 'different' [*diversum*].[14]

Now, near the beginning of Dante's *Purgatory* the narrator sees an angel steer a shipful of souls to land at the foot of the mountain of Purgatory, and the beginning of the same Psalm is quoted again.

> And near and nearer as he came full sail
>   The bird of God shone momently more bright,
>   So that mine eyes endured him not, but fell.
>
> And hard on toward the shore he steered his flight,
>   Borne forward in a ship that skimmed apace,
>   Drawing no water, 'twas so swift and light.

Freehold of bliss apparent in his face,
  The heavenly pilot on the poop stood tiptoe,
  And with him full an hundred souls had place.

'*In exitu Israel de Aegypto*',
  From end to end they sang their holy lay
  In unison; and so he brought the ship to.[15]

In his letter, Dante's choice of a text to elucidate the polysemy of his poem and at the same time exemplify received allegorical practice is, I think, significant. In the Western Church this Psalm was cited at liturgical moments of transition. It had its place in the last offices for the dying, its recitation accompanied the dead on their way to burial, and it was sometimes cited on the last Sunday before Advent at the end of one Church year and before the beginning of another. It was a paschal Psalm and was applied by the Church to the resurrection and was thus located at that crucial transitional moment in a Christian scheme of history (and in the time-scheme of the church's year) which both valorizes rereading the Old Testament as an analogue of the New, and, in terms of this interpretative programme, is also the moment particularly expected in the Old Testament texts. A text about deliverance was relevant in the rites of individual passage from one world to the next and to transitional Sundays in the liturgical calendar. Allegory, especially in the case of analogy, effects transitions of meaning. We have seen (in the Epistles) how exegesis was intent on typological anticipations of New Testament figures and events by those in the Old, and how transitions, rereadings and revalorizations were effected. Dante chooses a text about a narrative of transition (Israel's exodus from Egypt) to illustrate points about transitions of meaning, from one to the 'other' or to the 'different'. The word 'metaphor' itself originally contained the idea of transference, of carrying one thing to another. Metaphor, said Aristotle, is the application of a strange term (or even 'the name belonging to another', *onomatos allotriou*).[16] Another way of thinking of allegory is to see it situated on mutual boundaries or thresholds where many and different meanings touch and are produced. Like the senses elicited from Psalms 114:1–2 it is located in liminal moments.

In the narrative of his poem Dante similarly sites the verse at a coincidence of liminal moments and locations: at dawn, on a shore, at the foot of a mountain, between hell and purgatory proper, boundaries supervised by Cato, a pagan but also some sort of honorary Christian. As the boat itself is in transit, and before it reaches the shore, the text has embedded in the souls' song a Psalm fragment whose allegorical meanings elicited in the

letter to Can Grande can be seen as appropriate significations for
this moment in the poem. The *transit* of the boatload of souls
towards redemption here in his poetical fiction is Dante's own
analogue to Psalms 114:1 and its statement of the Jewish exodus.
Through this moment in the poem's own claim to analogy, in its
quotation of the verse, it explicitly lays a claim to such allegorical
meanings as those elicited in the letter. We could say (in the light
of the letter) that not only does Psalms 114:1 describe a type of
Christ's redemption of mankind, it is also a type of the scene
in *Purgatory* II. 37–48, which of course in turn theologically
assumes the analogical meaning which Dante's letter assigns to the
Psalm verse. This moment in the poem also represents particularly
the anagogic sense of what the passengers in the boat are singing:
they *are* the anagogic sense of what they sing.

One could extend exploration of the increasingly complex
generation and multiplication of meanings between all these texts.
As redeemed souls, perhaps the passengers are self-aware of the
allegorical significations of what they sing. Also, Dante is here
witnessing a passage to redemption which parallels his own journey
in the narrative: the souls' liminal transition is analogous to his
own at the foot of Mount Purgatory. Also, as writers since Horace
were fond of observing and quoting, for narrator and author (and
reader), *de te/Fabula narratur*: 'this story is also about you'.[17] I
suggested earlier that boundaries are appropriate metaphors for
the site of allegory, partly to avoid the stratification and hierarch-
ization implied in the metaphor popular for allegory of 'levels'.
(Which is the more important significance in the letter to Can
Grande: conversion from sin or the soul's release by death into
glory?). If 'boundaries' is an appropriate way of describing the site
occupied by allegory, then perhaps 'play' describes its operation,
especially the exchanges that go on between different texts in
allegory's production of significances, some of which are observable in the above two extracts from Dante and their possible
relations to each other.

It appears from our recent readings that earlier writers and
theorists of allegory assumed a world in which meaning is imma-
nent in all parts of that world. For them not only is allegory a
dimension of reading texts, but also texts have allegorical significations as they represent events, times, places, narratives, even
animals, that themselves have significations. Both the material
world (lions) and history itself (the exodus of the Jews from
Egypt) can be read allegorically to signify the redemption of
mankind.

I have spent some time examining Scriptural texts and passages of theory or poetry that have Scriptural texts embedded in them. Much of the history, theory and practice of early Western allegory stems from Biblical *exegesis*, that is, the explanation and interpretation of Scriptural texts. The Psalms, the Book of Revelation and the Epistles especially attracted the attention of centuries of exegetes, the Psalms being constantly interpreted from the earliest Christian times and the Epistles gaining a new prominence during the Reformation. Indeed, for many sixteenth-century readers like Erasmus, Paul in the Epistles was one of the greatest of the allegorizers.[18] The *Faerie Queene* opens with two figures which have analogues in the Epistles and which engage us in necessary acts of interpretation of them and in consideration of the play between texts, which I suggested as a figure for the operation of allegory. We as readers, and Spenser's Elizabethan Protestant poem, begin in a very Protestant way with attention to close reading and scrutiny of what is written, that is, with 'scripture'. The intense concern of the opening of the poem, and indeed much of the rest of Book I, is textual in all senses, as was that of the sixteenth-century humanists and religious reformers. That is, it is intensely concerned with texts and interpretations, particularly those of Scripture, and recognizes and appeals to their authority. The two figures we meet at the beginning have analogues in the Epistles, which were favourite texts for Protestantism and its interpretations. The place of interpretation in the context of sixteenth-century religious history will be addressed more fully in the next chapter. And not only do the two figural allegories at the beginning of Book I have Scriptural analogues, the whole of Book I is, among other things, a chivalric romance analogue to the last book of the Bible, Revelation, with its narratives of spiritual warfare. The Book of Revelation (written at the end of the first century AD) has a good claim to be the earliest example of sustained Christian allegory, and for some sixteenth-century writers it contained a summation of the truths of the whole Bible. Spenser has written in Book I a fiction in imitation of the fiction of the Apocalypse. Book I lays a claim to truth by grounding itself in the Book of Revelation. You may find it illuminating to read the twenty-two chapters of Revelation, so as to be able to see how some of the Apocalypse's figures, images and narratives are imitated in Book I. We will be looking at a section of it in the next chapter. Some writers on Spenser have noticed the parallels with the Apocalypse and you may find these helpful.[19]

In the case of the intertextualities between Psalm 114, Dante's letter to Can Grande, and a passage in *Purgatory* II, we saw that the four traditional senses of Scripture were some of the significances available. As both Dante and Aquinas observe, these were given various names, but the division was usually a large one into literal and allegorical, with the further division of allegorical into analogical,[20] moral (also called tropological) and anagogical: we have seen these exemplified in Dante's letter. Similarly, the narrative of *Faerie Queene*, Book I, being analogical to Revelation, these traditional allegorical senses may be signified by the 'literal' or the 'historical' narrative. In the early seventeenth century a man who claimed to be a friend of Spenser's saw in Book I the working-out of such a fourfold life of man.[21] But also, as in the case of the Dante texts, significances will certainly not exhaust themselves in four senses: allegorical play will continue between them.

3. Misreading

'. . . Interpretation is nothing but the possibility of error . . .'
(Paul de Man, *Blindness and Insight* 1971, p. 141)

The texts we looked at at the end of the last chapter were confident in their positions on allegory. Though the interpretation of literary or even material allegories might be cryptic and complex, it did not appear problematic. The texts were optimistic about the reliability of the relation of words to meanings, of signifiers to signifieds: a verse in Psalms about the exodus of the Jews serenely yielding the redemption of mankind, moral conversion, and death as liberation into glory as successive meanings. Those texts on allegory assumed that a sign is a true token of some fact or quality, or is a thing substituting truthfully for something else.

But there is a long history of critical anxiety that representations may deceive, from Plato to Renaissance defenders of fiction who still felt an urgent need to answer this anxiety in their treatises. That the relationship of representation to truth is not always reliable or direct has already been our primary experience in the opening stanzas of Book I of the *Faerie Queene*, in both the representations of the knight (signs that led to errors of assumption) and of the lady (signs that veil truthfulness). Our early experiences in reading the *Faerie Queene* were of misreading. Signs may speak truthfully, but what if a sign could be described not as a truthful substitution but as something which can be used in order to lie, for 'if something cannot be used to tell a lie, conversely it cannot be used to tell the truth'?[1] Book I is concerned with its own and allegory's relation to truth, and how far we can be sure of either. Its immediate concern in its narrative will logically be with successive moments of deception. Allegory, you will remember from the letter to Can Grande, is so called because its Greek root means 'other' or 'different'. So mustn't allegory's attempts at representation always be misrepresentations? In the act of substituting, hasn't allegory, in the words of Swift's rational Houyhnhnms, 'said the thing which is not'? Like metaphor, allegory paradoxically and simultaneously asserts identity *and* difference. And what if the tendency of allegory to generate a cornucopian succession of meanings (as we saw in the Dante texts and the bestiary) becomes promiscuous, and Aquinas' carefully permitted objection ('Allow a variety of readings to one passage, and you produce confusion and deception...') escapes the safe parameters of the Thomist question and grows a serious and monstrous threat? And what if the allegorical sign is susceptible to contradictory readings? The author of the bestiary tells us that the signified of a lion cub is the risen Christ, and cites Revelation 5:5 on Christ as the lion of Judah's tribe. A text he does not cite, for obvious reasons, is one from the Epistles: 'Awake! be on the alert! Your enemy the devil, like a roaring lion, prowls round looking for someone to devour' (1 Peter 5:8, Revised Version).

Let us locate these theoretical problems about representation in the *Faerie Queene*, Book I. First, let us take a section of the narrative. **Look again at I i–ii, paying particular attention to i 36–ii 9 and looking especially closely at i 45–6. What is the actual sequence of events? Write out an account of these events in your own words. What bearing do the events at night in the magician's house in I i–ii have on our discussion about representation and misrepresentation? What relation do the various 'sights', seen by the knight, particularly those created by magic, have to this issue?**

DISCUSSION

Perhaps you had some of the same problems as I did in being clear about what happens in this section. The narrative is one of confusing events for both knight and reader. I find it difficult to keep track exactly of the activities of the spirits raised by the magician, the operation of the dreams, whether the knight is asleep or awake. Particularly difficult is deciding which spirit does what. So it is both comforting and revealing to find that Spenser's most eminent modern editor says (I think, mistakenly) that 'that false other Spright' at I ii 3.2 is the dream,[2] when it is surely one of the two spirits originally raised at i 38. I think (but am not *entirely* sure) that the events of the night are as follows. The magician raises two spirits: let us call them A and B. A is sent on an errand, B remains with the magician to await his commands (i 38.6–9). A descends to the house of Morpheus, the god of sleep, finds Morpheus asleep, wakes him and returns to the magician bearing on its wings a false dream (i 39–44). Meanwhile the magician takes spirit B and makes an aerial body for it which gives it the appearance of the lady (45–47). A places itself at the knight's head and, interfering with his sleeping imagination, gives him disturbing erotic dreams, even that his lady is in bed with him, depending on whether we interpret 'by him lay' (47.7) as 'in the same room' or 'in the same bed'. The knight then dreams, in a confusing reversal of time-sequence if he thinks the lady is in bed with him, that the lady is brought to his bed. He starts up (is he really awake after 49.1–4?) apparently to find to his horror that his dream comes true and his lady is in his bedroom. She speaks passionately and tearfully of her unfulfilled desire for him. He is suspicious but courteously comforts her (51–54) and falls into a troubled sleep (55). Spirit B as lady and the dream return to the magician. In a second attempt on the knight the magician takes the disguised spirit B and disguises spirit A (not the dream) as a Squire. He lays them both in a bed and wakes the knight to see them. Deceived and enraged by the false show the knight wants to kill the seeming lovers. He returns to bed and after a restless night leaves the magician's house as the dawn breaks, believing his lady unfaithful.

As my attempts at paraphase admit, the narrative of events is sufficiently complicated, but I find the method of narration makes the task of deciphering it clearly even more difficult. Why is this?

For one thing, isn't there constant duplication and repetition in personages, events and situations? To deceive the knight the magician chooses *two* spirits. Their duplicity is manifested syntactically in the stanza in which they first appear in antitheses and appositions ('To aide ... or fray', 'The one ... The other' 'two, the falsest twoo' i 38.5–9), and rhetorically in the oxymoron (brief figure of speech composed of two contradictory terms) 'true-seeming lyes' where the qualifying compound adjective is both double in its form and signifies duplicity in its meaning. The oxymoron proposes the problem of distinguishing truth from lies by bringing truth and lies closely together, but inserting between them the possibility of misrepresenting lies as truth in 'seeming'. Doubleness itself seems to constitute falseness in this section. I find in the dictionary that 'double-dealing' is both the usual and earliest sense of 'duplicity', not the more innocent sense of simply 'the state of being numerically double'. When the 'two' are chosen, 'two' makes its appearance in a line together with a statement of superlative falseness, and doubleness is immediately qualified by an apposition which defines two as superlatively false and immediately repeats, duplicates the number itself, 'he chose out two, the falsest twoo' (i 38.7).

What I find confusing in the episodes is that there appear to be two of everything, and it is difficult to keep these doubles distinct because of their similarity and their tendency to blur into each other. We have already experienced the difficulty of keeping the two spirits distinguished. The antithesis that should keep them apart ('The one of them . . . The other . . .', 38.8–9) is usually used either without referents or immediate context, or the pairing is left incomplete, so 'the one' and 'the other' are useless as indications of exactly which spirit is being referred to. Let us trace in I i–ii the repetition of these motifs, especially that of duplicity, which we discover in i 38.

Bewildering duplications continue. One of the two spirits, unhelpfully referred to simply as 'he' (39.1) is sent to Morpheus, passing through double gates of silver and ivory which repeat the antithesis characteristic of the two spirits ('The one . . . The other', 40.2–3). Morpheus is asleep, thus literalizing his personification as god of dreams and also duplicating the state of the knight. His disturbed sleep (42.7–9) both reflects the contemporary but undescribed disturbance of the knight's sleep and anticipates a disturbance that the narrative will describe (55.5–7). Morpheus is a sort of personification of the state of dreaming, that is, he is an allegorical trope of dreaming. When he is shaken, the poem dizzyingly describes him as *like* a man in a dream (42.7–9). A personification of dreams (and a personification of the knight's dreaming) being figuratively like a dreaming man, is an instance where the fiction of the poem's narrative and its figurative language begin to collapse into each other. If we return to Aristotle's definition of a metaphor (the application to one thing of the name of something else) then what threatens to happen in the case of the knight and Morpheus is the erosion of the separating distinction that enables metaphor to work. There is threatened the collapse of metaphor which literary theorists from Quintilian to Puttenham regarded as the most widely employed, beautiful and powerful instance of figurative language: 'There is no trope more florishing than a metaphore'.[3] This collapse is particularly unsettling if allegory as trope is an expanded metaphor.

Meanwhile, back at the hermitage . . . We are reminded of B, the other false spirit, only long enough to watch it fashioned into a false likeness. This deliberate duplication and misrepresentation is crucially important as it misrepresents the figure whom we and the knight relied on as an accurate representation of truth. At exactly that moment when her false double appears, the lady is named as Una: one, single, unchanging, unique. We as readers are privileged as witnesses of the moment of duplication and as receptors of the naming which happens unobtrusively at the very end of the stanza (45.9). The falseness of duplication continues as the magician's construction of the false Una closely imitates the poem's own first description of Una we looked at earlier (cf. 45 with 4).

This is a subtle instance of doubling and imitation. But we as alert readers are in a good position to distinguish true from false fiction in that we witness the totality of the poem's events (cf Chapter 1, pp. 4–6). We see the 'artes', 'witt' and 'guile' of the maker's artifice, words which bear traces of old anxieties about skilful but deceitful representation. Having seen the manufacture of the double, we will have an advantage over the knight when it comes to telling it apart from the real. As Una is named to distinguish her from her duplicate, so the actual similarity (but not identity) may serve to distinguish the true from the false. That is, it may serve to preserve the sense of likeness *and* difference which is essential to figurative language, particularly metaphor, and to the reading of allegory. **How does i 45–6 compare with i 4? How are the two Unas dressed? How do they conduct themselves?**

DISCUSSION

Una conceals herself with a black stole, the magician throws a black stole over her duplicate. The double is without the important veil that conceals Una's face and also draws attention to her concealed truthfulness.[4] Una's layered self-concealments (cloak over veil over whiteness) veil truth: the false Una's black stole conceals only a metaphor for painful entrapment ('her bayted hooke', 49.6). Indeed, as opposed to Una's concealment of her face, the double advertises her charms and they are deployed to such good effect that her maker is almost beguiled. Her face is

on display to the knight in her amorous complaint to him (51–4).
In terms of likeness and resemblance, the false duplicate is representation detached from what it should represent. 'So lively, and
so like in all men's sight' can mean many things, 'so animated and
so lifelike' being one of them, but as a reader I can't help feeling
that 'like' is left dangling in the line: 'and so like *what*?', I find
myself asking as I wait for a statement of the thing it is like which
never comes, leaving me with a sense of pure likeness, of representation without meaning, of emptied resemblance.

These stanzas, then, raise questions of the untruthfulness of
some representations. The repetition of 'maker' as a term for the
magician as producer of the false Una (45.6, 46.7) calls to mind
the common use of this word in the sixteenth century for 'poet'.[5]
The magician's art is analogous to the poet's: both may deceive
in their representations. How far we are prepared to approve
concealment from us or our own deception, how far these might
be benevolent, and under what circumstances dangerous or
vicious, are questions the poem asks here, and ones you should
keep constantly in mind in reading Spenser's poem. Is Una entitled
to conceal but not her duplicate? Why?

Given our examination of the doubleness of both representation and misrepresentation, the view of Spenser's contemporary
George Puttenham's 'Of Figures and figurative speeches' is illuminating and apt. He says that they

> be occupied of purpose to deceive the eare and also the minde,
> drawing it from plainnesse and simplicitie to a certain doublenesse,
> whereby our talke is the more guilefull & abusing, for what else is
> your *Metaphor* but an inversion of sence by transport; your *allegorie*
> by a duplicitie of meaning or dissimulation under covert and dark
> intendments.[6]

Confusing duplications continue in these episodes. Who are 'they'
in 47.1? The familiar antithesis, 'The one . . .', is promised in 47.3,
but the other never appears in this stanza or immediately succeed-
ing ones. 'The one' is presumably the spirit who went on the
mission to Morpheus. Is the dream the knight has at 47.4 the
dream that this spirit carried back on its wings (44.8)? If not,
what happened to it? Who is 'she' in 48.1? Venus? Una? (that
is, the appearance of Una, or rather the appearance of Una in
a dream). Ironically the most radically uncertain and unsettling
word in this line (even its exact grammatical status could be in
doubt) is 'self', which ought to function to re-emphasize identity.
Between 'she' in 48.1 and 'her' in 48.3 is poised a series of phrases
in potential apposition to 'she', 'her' and each other: 'her selfe', 'of

beautie soueraigne Queene', 'Faire *Venus*'. Again in this stanza
comparisons are announced, but at the same time the two terms
involved in the comparison are difficult to distinguish as they
dissolve into each other. I do not think that the poem or its author
are confused, but they do want us to experience some of the
knight's confusion. They also want us to realize something about
the possibilities of deception in representation of which the author
of the poem, in his writing of fiction and his use of metaphor and
allegory, is keenly aware.

In a nightmarish moment the knight wakes and finds to
his horror his dream appears to be true. True to the episode's
articulation of duplicity there are actually two false Unas; in the
demonically induced dream and now a disguised spirit. Rage gives
way to a desire to test. 'He stayde his hand, and gan himselfe
aduise/To proue his sense, and tempt her faigned truth.' This is a
wonderfully ambiguous construction. A simple paraphrase would
be 'he gave consideration to testing the evidence of his senses,
and put to the test her pretended honesty'. These lines (50.5–6)
incorporate *our* perception of the presence of a falsehood (false
Una) that ought to be tested, but also admit to what is already
here the knight's unspoken assumption that the *real* Una is false. If
the knight assumed Una's 'truth', he would not think her fidelity
'faigned' and wish now to test it. His unspoken assumption here
is the exact opposite of the true case. He now assumes that
the real Una's fidelity to him is pretended, on the evidence of the
behaviour of another who *is* pretending to be truth. The false Una
gives ample examples of linguistic duplicity in 51–52, in her
constant tired doubling of phrases in 52.5–7 where the doublets
in each line are paired by alliteration, assonance and repetition.
Notice especially the excessive alliteration of the letter *f* – and try
saying these lines aloud:

> Captiu'd to *f*ortune and *f*rayle worldly *f*eares,
> *F*ly to your *f*aith for *s*uccour and *s*ure ayde:
> *L*et me not dye in *l*angour and *l*ong teares.

She even untruthfully starts a false duplicate rewriting of the
poem's story, for she claims that love was the prime motive for
her leaving her father's kingdom (52.1–2) whereas we know that
the true Una's departure was enforced by the dragon (5.7–9).

The final intensified and successfully deceiving duplications
are wittily delayed until after the break between Cantos i and ii
and the second part of the night. The second assault reduplicates
the first: the manufacture of another aerial body repeats i 45–46.
The false Squire in bed with false Una replicates the knight's

dream in i 47, with the Squire replacing the knight. The new couple in ii 3–5 are doubly false: they are neither Una nor a Squire, and they are only impersonating spirits, not humans. At last 'that false other Spright' returns, but spirit A is now the false 'other' and terms that ought to keep them apart only serve further to confuse them. There is another duplication in that the knight turns again to a restless night as he did at the end of Canto i.

By ii 6 the knight is separated from single truthfulness, that is, from Una. In ii 9 Archimago sees his guests 'diuided into double parts' and in a another act of duplication puts on the appearance of the knight. As the false Una's manufacture rewrote the real Una's initial description, so ii 11 rewrites the first stanza of the poem and its details. Some duplications increase irony in both ii 11 and i 1: 'Full iolly knight he seemde' (i i.8, ii 11.7). The inner man of ii 11 greatly increases our sense of incongruity there between inner man and enclosing armour, and ironically recalls that first incongruity in i 1.

I think that one of the episode's significances concerns the production of representations; specifically the significance of the first of a series of false duplicates in the narrative of Book I, more generally of fictions and Puttenham's 'Figures and figurative speeches'. The poem has witnessed the advent of false others and substitutions which we may read allegorically as signifying the duplicitous ability 'to speake one thing and mean another' of metaphor, allegory and indeed irony. To quote Puttenham again, 'To be short, every speach wrested from his owne naturall signification . . . is a kinde of dissimulation'.[7] The knight who had earlier triumphed, with Una's help, over an obviously foul personification of misinterpretation in Error, succumbs to a misreading of more subtle duplicity. As he parts from Una we as readers have to detach ourselves from his now inadequate perception and ability to read his world. We shared his confusion in Archimago's house, but reject his rash conclusion that Una is false. His ability to read signs will prove inadequate in his next encounter.

Although, as I said earlier, I will now and again turn in this *Guide* to close formalist reading of passages, I want also to address larger critical issues about Spenser's poem and suggest how the poem might respond to different kinds of critical approach. Deconstructive, historical and feminist readings of passages will be briefly introduced in this chapter. Through another instance of intertextuality, we will try to contextualize our present general issues of (mis)readings, falseness and misrepresentation within sixteenth-century history, that is, to historicize them. We will then

turn to some basic feminist approaches which arise from our
discussions so far. But first we will briefly continue to look at the
issue of reading and of viewpoint in this poem. **Read Canto ii,
paying particular attention to ii 12–14. What (or whose) viewpoint is implied in these stanzas? How does Redcrosse (named at
ii 15.1) read Duessa (conclusively identified as such at ii 44.1)
particularly in 13–14? Do you think that your interpretation of
Duessa differs from what we assume to be his?**

DISCUSSION

The viewpoint of ii 12–14 is difficult to establish. The move
in location and viewpoint from Archimago falsely disguised as
Redcrosse to Redcrosse takes place between ii 11 and ii 12. Here
is ii 12:

> But he the knight, whose semblaunt he did beare,
> The true *Saint George* was wandred far away,
> Still flying from his thoughts and gealous feare;
> Will was his guide, and griefe led him astray.
> At last him chaunst to meete vpon the way
> A faithlesse Sarazin all arm'd to point,
> In whose great shield was writ with letters gay
> *Sans foy*: full large of limbe and euery joint
> He was, and cared not for God or man a point.

In ii 12 we return from the poem's account of Archimago to
Redcrosse as an observer and narrative viewpoint oddly defined as
absent and wandering, or as a 'he' constituted only as an appearance ('semblaunt', 12.1) now appropriated by Archimago. What
is happening to Redcrosse in the poem opens up the text to
a deconstructive approach. Deconstructive criticism flowered in
the early 1970s. It doubts fixed meaning in language and sees
traditional Western philosophical concerns with certainty and
truth as repressing the instability of language. A central deconstructive idea is that language postpones fixed and certain meaning (truth, identity, authenticity) along an endless chain where a
final truth is endlessly deferred and absent. Redcrosse, as he is
constituted in ii 12, is an example of the deconstructive principle
that 'the structure of the sign is determined by the trace or track of
that other which is forever absent'.[8] Redcrosse's true identity
is receding (Una will later describe him as 'of your selfe...
berobbed', viii 42.8). Indeed, I think that it started receding
after his wilful self-separation and flight from truth in Una. It is

possible to imagine 12.2 as a parenthesis, that is, Redcrosse's identity as St George (later confirmed at x 61) has wandered from the knight himself who is defined only as a 'semblaunt'. So perhaps Archimago's impersonation is therefore an ironically truer likeness of Redcrosse now than we first realize. Lines 5–6 distance themselves and us from his wilfulness and error, and make him the object, not the subject, of his next encounter ('him chaunst'), which is with a knight whose presentation ironically recalls Redcrosse's own at the beginning of the poem. The recollection is apt: Redcrosse, too, is faithless like Sansfoy ('without faith'). This rapid multiplication of ironies in the poem is one aspect of the doubleness of representation considered above. Irony is a mode which does 'likewise dissemble'.[9]

Redcrosse's viewpoint is available, but problematic (we no longer trust his judgement and he is no longer 'true' to himself). So is Sansfoy's. Readers have access to both and can also read Duessa building on or dissenting from both. Who 'sees' Duessa in 13–14? Complexity of reading has increased greatly since the opening of the poem, where access to Redcrosse and Una was direct and relatively unmediated. **What do we make of Duessa?**

DISCUSSION

It is difficult to say. Duessa is apparently attractive ('faire', 'goodly'), striking in her bright red and jewels, exotic in her Persian mitre, amorous, sparkling and tinkling. She is entertaining and diverting. Perhaps as readers who have been exercised so much by appearances we are least wary of the portrait's attention to externals and surfaces. Even 'faire' and 'goodly' need commit themselves to no more than appearance, as we realized in a temporary uncertainty about the application of 'faire' to Una (i 4.1). This is yet another duplication of Una. As we have found Redcrosse replicated by both Archimago and Sansfoy, so Una is doubly replicated by the false duplicate and now by Duessa. For Duessa reproduces the initial mode of representation of Una: fair companion to knight, mount, description of clothes, attention to demeanour. In view of later events, 'faire' and 'goodly' are used ironically of Duessa. I think that we still have a sense of the clichés Spenser is elaborating. Una's black and white suggest simple definitions of good and evil and also the idea of plain, obvious and unmistakable truth ('there it is, in black and white'). Compared with Una's sober black and white, Duessa's brightness is gaudy. She is 'a scarlet woman'.

Duessa's portrait in Spenser's poem is an analogue to a woman described at the opening of Revelation 17, and is a particularly good and sharp instance of Spenser's imitation of a moment from the Apocalypse. Among the interesting things revealed by the comparison are some not presently explicit at this moment in the poem.

. . . I will shew thee the damnation of the great [1] whore . . .

So he caried mee away into the wildernesse in the Spirite, and I sawe a woman sit upon a scarlet coloured [2] beast, full of names of [3] blasphemie, which had seven heads, and ten hornes.

And the [4] woman was arayed in purple and skarlet, and guilded with golde, and precious stones, and pearles, and had a cup of golde in her hand, full of [5] abominations, and filthinesse of her fornication.

And in her forehead was a name written, [6] A mysterie, great Babylon, the mother of whoredomes, and abominations of the earth.

[1] Antichrist is compared to an harlot, because he seduceth the world with vaine wordes, doctrines of lies, and outward appearances.
[2] The beast signifieth the ancient Rome: the woman that sitteth thereon, the newe Rome which is the Papistrie, whose crueltie and bloodshedding is declared by scarlet.
[3] Full of idolatrie, superstition and contempt of the true God.
[4] This woman is the Antichrist, that is, the Pope with the whole body of his filthie creatures, as is expounded, Vers. 18 whose beautie onely standeth in outward pompe and impudencie, and craft like a strumpet.
[5] Of false doctrines and blasphemies.
[6] Which none can know to avoide, but the elect.

How does this passage affect our reading of Duessa? Having read it, what sense do you get of a sixteenth-century Protestant's view of the Church of Rome?

DISCUSSION

The intertextual relationships between the initial portrait of Duessa and the Geneva Bible's description in biblical text and marginal glosses of the great whore Babylon is more complex than

that between the portrait of Redcrosse and the Christian soldier of
Ephesians we looked at in Chapter 1. Geneva's marginals read
the whore not only as Antichrist, but more specifically as the
antichristian papacy. This exegesis is particular and historical. The
figural allegory is not subjected just to a general moral reading,
as seductive, outward, lying beauty concealing inner filth of
falsity and cruelty. This is thought characteristic of antichristian
deception, and such a nexus of wickedness is located for the
sixteenth-century English Protestant reader in the papacy. The
perspective of the exegesis is also historical in that the cruelty and
bloodshed of the historical institution of the papacy repeat and
perpetuate in modern history the cruelty and bloodshed of a
previous and analogous antichristian institution, the Roman
empire.

On the basis of this passage sixteenth-century Protestants
saw the Roman church as seductive, deceiving, cruel, idolatrous,
superstitious, showy, superficial, attractive, false and blasphemous.
A reading of the portrait of Duessa in conjunction with her
imitated original, Babylon, and the gloss's identification of Babylon
as the Roman Church, reveals them all as apparently beautiful,
splendidly and exquisitely dressed, exotic, adorned, promiscuous,
showy, glittering, entertaining, fickle. The representation of
Duessa in I ii 13–14 carries the impression of a sixteenth-century
English Protestant view of the Roman Church. Information about
sixteenth-century religious history, controversy and propaganda
consolidates and extends our reading of Duessa. We could identify
and begin to map polysemous allegorical meanings at play in her
portrait, ranging from generalized morality to historical particu-
larity: duplicitous seductive show, the show of a seductive but
false religion, the false attractiveness of Roman Catholicism for
a sixteenth-century English reader. Formalist reading uncovered
the concern of the opening two cantos with truth, falsity, representation and misrepresentation: simple historical contextual-
ization reveals something of the particular configurations of these
issues in sixteenth-century religious conflicts.

When we looked at the opening descriptions of Redcrosse
and the veiled Una together with passages from the Epistles to
which they are related, I emphasized my feeling that to recognize
more and fuller readings was not to end reading. I suppose that
what I had to say at the end of the last chapter about allegory saw
plenitude and multiplicity of interpretation as functions of its
operation. Remember, too, Hamilton's thoughts on genuineness
of reading going together with incompleteness of reading. We
may now, for the moment, be reading Duessa historically with

sixteenth-century eyes as a figure for the Roman church, but we should not think this reading the final or the most important one.

The poem has so far offered representations of truth and falsehood; the former in Una, the latter in her duplicates, the false Una and Duessa, and in the bipartite female hybrid Error. The constitution of truth is seen as a binary opposition, that is, in terms of paired opposites which are related to each other and therefore serve to define each other. This opposition is manifested in opposing female representations who, as we have seen, are nevertheless linked in their mode of presentation. This is the point at which to ask, very generally for the moment, some feminist questions of the poem. Is it possible to recognize feminine experience in an apparently masculine genre, chivalric romance epic? Or does the poem illustrate the way literature has often constructed women as 'other', abnormal, deviant. Or might there be more positive female images visible or recoverable from the poem? That is, is the poem open to or resistant to various feminist readings?[10] In terms of the poem's fictional figures, hasn't the narrative predominantly offered us the point of view of the knight?

Try giving an account of the narrative of the first two cantos of the *Faerie Queene* from Una's point of view. How does it differ from our account so far? As yet we have not progressed very far into Book I's narrative, but you could try the following exercises on passages you will come across later. What do you make of the description of the 'mayden Queene' at I iv 7–12? What do you think that this passage has to say about female rulers? Does it approve of them? Can there be any justification of the description of the poem's stripping and exposure of the female body in the terms in which this is done at I viii 45–50? What sort of picture of femininity is offered to us in Charissa (I x 30–31)?

DISCUSSION

I will only outline a few suggestions as a basis for thinking about some of these questions. Una's perception of the Error episode, for example, would be very different. Some reasons for this were touched on in Chapter 1 (pp. 3–4). And Truth is asleep and absent during Redcrosse's many errors and misperceptions in the hermitage of Archimago and after, and is not faced with the same problems as the fallible Redcrosse. What I iv 7–12 has to say about female rulers is a tricky question and one to which I will return below (pp. 57–8). In answer to the question about

I viii 45–50, one could say that Spenser strips Duessa allegorically
to reveal the foulness of falsehood. But is it essential to his purpose to excite disgust particularly in relation to her female sexual
characteristics? The fact that this is a vivid symbolic representation of the filthiness of falsehood, and particularly that of the
Roman Church, might only be an evasion. To say that the
representation here is decorous as it is in proportion to a hatred
of falsehood might be another evasion. Isn't the moral disgust
directed more at the female representation than at the abstraction
or institution of which it is a personification? Here is a brief
passage from a commentator on the Apocalypse in 1644, working
himself up into a lather at the thought of the Babylonian Whore,
the Church of Rome:

> see this impudent harlot at length slit in the nostrils, stripped of her
> garments and tires [attire], besmeared with dirt and rotten eggs, and
> at last burnt up and consumed with fire.[11]

Isn't the language and feeling here comparable with that in the
stripping of Duessa and might it not share in the same cultural
misogyny?

   Feminist issues arising from Spenser's poem are being increasingly addressed by critics. It is obviously far too early in our
reading of the poem to attempt any conclusion, but since issues of
truth and falsehood, crucial to the narrative and significance of
Book I and to allegory in general, are proposed by the poem at its
inception in terms of female representations, some of the issues,
which I will take up later particularly in relation to Book III, may
be briefly raised here.

   Are we to take the view that the poem assumed/assumes a
male readership and offers reading pleasures, including objects
of desire, to men rather than women? Doesn't the account of
Redcrosse's disturbed night imply a masculine psychology and set
of values? Is there, in short, a position for women readers in this
text?[12] But, at least at the time of the publication of the poem's
first three books in 1590, the title-page (see Penguin edition, p. 37)
publically directs Spenser's poetic labours primarily to a female
addressee, Elizabeth I. The queen is invoked, too, in various
female aspects, in the Proem to the whole work and is often
addressed directly or indirectly in the course of the poem.[13]
Spenser's dedicatory sonnets (Penguin edition, pp. 25–33)[14] pre-
ponderantly address powerful male aristocrats as readers, but
the last three address the Countess of Pembroke (defined as Sir
Philip Sidney's sister), Lady Carew, and ladies at court, the latter
group perhaps suggesting an implied communal female audience.

Although there is a preponderance of male dedicatees of these sonnets they might also suggest an implied readership limited by social class rather than gender. The male poet Spenser, in a letter to a powerful male patron, Sir Walter Ralegh (Penguin edition, pp. 15–18), tells him that the general end of the poem is 'to fashion a gentleman or noble person in vertuous and gentle discipline' (p. 15). A gentleman is undeniably male, but is 'noble person' merely in apposition to gentleman, or might it be female as well as male? Many examples of heroism offered in the letter are male (Agamemnon, Ulysses, Orlando, Godfredo, p. 15), but there are to be female representations, too, of the queen (the Faery Queen herself, Belphoebe) and of heroism (Britomart, p. 16).

What of the female characters depicted in the poem so far: do they offer positive or negative images of women? Do they offer points of engagement for female readers and interpretations? I have said that the dominant viewpoint in the poem so far has been that of the male protagonist of Book I, the Redcrosse knight. On the other hand, you and I as readers have seen that *his* ability to read is already severely inadequate, and as readers we have already detached ourselves from it as exclusive or reliable, and are in the process of improvising another. The poem is encouraging us to an overview that cannot simply be that of Redcrosse. The poem's male knight-reader is imperceptive about the poem's embodiment of truth in Una. The poem chooses female representations for the important construction of truth and its opposites. But this, in turn, is open to a more subtle criticism, that so far in Book I the poem constructs woman as either the fairest truth or the foulest deceit, as either angel or monster. On the one hand Una, on the other Duessa, false Una, Error. And these polarities (chastity, purity, honesty; lasciviousness, foulness, deceitfulness) may have in common, and be related to each other as, equally distorted images of the feminine.[15] As such, female figures so far in the *Faerie Queene* are only offered as alternative images of the angel and the witch. I think that a possible rejoinder is that at least truth assumes a female form, even at the expense of error and deceit assuming forms of female monstrosity. Truth and the best reading are certainly not located in the wilful and erring male knight. Do you think, then, that the interpretative space in the poem created by disassociation from fallible male knight, and the mutual unsatisfactoriness of the subject position (point of view) of the reader as beautiful female truth and monstrous female falsehood, allows equal occupation by women and men readers? We will have to re-examine this question as we read further into the poem.

4. Structure and Narrative in Book I

'... so in they entred arre.'

(*Faerie Queene*, I i 7.9)

So far I have been dealing with issues arising from reading the early parts of Book I, with representation in language, and with some preliminary thoughts about allegory. In this chapter we will look at the organization of Book I's narrative and then at the way large structural patterns order its arrangement of characters and ideas. There are many ways in which the form of Book I and the articulation of its narrative have been and can be described and accounted for, at least in part. I have glanced at two of these in the previous two chapters: apocalyptic patterns and their interpretation, and Reformation versions of the history of the Church. Some of the other ways in which critics have thought of its structure are as the story of man's Fall and its consequences, as the legend of St George, in terms of numerological patterns (that is, a structure based on beliefs about numbers), and in terms of parallels to contemporary and recent events in the sixteenth century. If you would like a taste now of these and other ideas about influences shaping Book I's narrative, the note at the end of this sentence will direct you to some samples.[1] Alternatively, you may wish to wait until after you have worked with this chapter of the *Guide*, which will begin to work on the structure of Book I, and then go back to consider again some of the ideas in Chapter 3.

First, you should read Book I all the way through, attending to its

story, or rather its several stories. You will probably find it helpful to make notes, or even draw simple diagrams of its events, major figures and locations. Spenser's narrative is lengthy, his descriptions elaborate, the persons in Book I many, and without notes readers of Spenser (myself included) would find it very difficult to remember the exact order of events. Even campaign-hardened Spenserians might be floored by a question like 'For which Saracen does Duessa seek the help of Night, and when?', let alone 'In which canto?', or even 'Why?' Nor need you read Book I all at one sitting. Take rests where there seems to you to be a natural pause in the narrative. You should take note of where these pauses occur, or where the narrator, drawing attention to himself and the activity of his own story-telling, comments on a different turn in events, shifts the focus in his narrative, changes the tone or style.

It is a large question to ask, but what sense do you get of the general outline of the story of Book I? What do you expect, from the early stages of the poem, in the way of a story, and what do you actually get in the course of Book I? A story usually has a beginning, a middle and an end. Can you briefly say what each of these is in Book I?

DISCUSSION

I think that what we expect of Book I is the fulfilment of the programme of narrative expectations briefly outlined in the poem's first five stanzas and most concisely in I i 3: Redcrosse's quest, given him by the Faery Queen herself, to kill the dragon and free Una's parents. If we have even a vague recollection of the story of George and the dragon, or any of its many analogues in European myth and fairy-tales, we know the story of knight-fights-monster-gets-girl. And indeed this is what we do eventually get, but not until I xi and xii. A simple narrative diagnosis and prognosis for Book I is offered in i 3:

(A) Departure or origin/the giving of the errand by Gloriana.
(B) The journey or quest ('and euer as he rode'); what happens in between, and how you get from A to C.
(C) Arrival or end/the killing of the horrible enemy who is the dragon, which will result in the knight's winning of honour and the grace of the Faery Queen.

We start with A and eventually we get to C; but it is B that takes up most of the first book of the *Faerie Queene* and it is full of all sorts of things we might not have predicted at the outset: digressions, interruptions which divert knight, narrative and

reader from the quest to kill the dragon. As we have seen in
Chapter 3 of this *Guide*, the knight who started out in I i accompanied by a beautiful woman and charged with a quest to kill
a dragon is at the end of I ii already going in a different direction,
accompanied by a completely different woman, and has apparently
forgotten all about the dragon.

**Of what kind are the interruptions, digressions, diversions which
slow down the narrative and impede the end we expect?**

DISCUSSION

Not only is the story of Redcrosse's quest delayed by his taking up
with Duessa, it is also interrupted by extended descriptions of
places and buildings, and by other stories in the shape of narrative
digressions. Descriptive set-pieces punctuate and halt the narrative:
the House of Pride (I iv) and the House of Celia (I x) are the ones
which come to mind first. And Book I is full of characters telling
each other and us their stories. Fradubio (ii 31ff), Prince Arthur
(ix 2ff), Trevisan (ix 25ff) are some examples: can you remember
others? Duessa is the earliest and most mendacious instance
(ii 22ff). And there are digressions within digressions. In I v Duessa
seeks help for the wounded Sansjoy. This leads to the encounter
with Night and the descent to the underworld to seek the help of
Aesculapius, which involves the further digression of the story of
Hippolytus (37–40), a mythological figure who does not actually
appear in the narrative of the *Faerie Queene* at all. This section
of I v is a chain of proliferating digressions, and inside these
digressions are also the set-piece descriptions of a descent to the
underworld and of the captives in the House of Pride.

I realize that when I wrote earlier in this chapter of 'the story'
in Book I, I might have suggested imprecisely that there is only
one narrative line, whereas there are two for the first half of Book
I. In Chapter 3 we considered the divisions and duplications of
the night in Archimago's house. For some time after that the
two stories of Redcrosse and Una go their separate ways: his is
followed in Cantos ii, iv, v and hers in Cantos iii and vi. Canto vii
tells us of both, and the pair are reunited in Canto viii and travel
together again to the end of the book. So, as you may have
noticed, the first six cantos of the book tell two stories of the
separated and divided Redcrosse and Una and the second six bring
them together. Redcrosse's story and Book I are divided into two
by the coming of Arthur, whose portrait (I vii 29–36) roughly
separates the sections of I vii concerned with Redcrosse and Una.
So we have two main narrative lines in Book I. I find it useful to

think of these two narratives of Redcrosse and Una in the first half of the book in a musical metaphor, as counterpointing each other, that is, as two melodies which may be different and separate, but accompany and sometimes imitate and comment on each other.

Let us look at this in more detail. Can you think of ways in which the two stories of Redcrosse and Una 'counterpoint' each other, that is of ways in the first six cantos in which the stories parallel but also differ from and perhaps comment on each other?

DISCUSSION

There are some obvious similarities – they both wander divided from each other and encounter individuals, dwellings and communities. Redcrosse, of course, takes up with Duessa, fights Sansfoy and Sansjoy, encounters Fradubio, visits the House of Pride, and is eventually imprisoned in Orgoglio's castle in Canto vii. Una, deserted by Redcrosse, goes in search of him, encounters the lion and is rescued by Satyrane, stays one night in the cottage of Abessa and Corceca and for a long time with the satyrs. The obvious differences, too, are clear. Redcrosse faithlessly flees Una but she faithfully seeks him. The knight's career is punctuated by a series of successful chivalric contests until he loses hopelessly in the fight with Orgoglio. Una repeatedly needs protection and rescue in her wanderings. Her need for protection is itself an ironic criticism of Redcrosse. Her proper protector, the knight, is absent, has abandoned her and is fighting for Duessa. You can find both the narrator and Una ruminating on the ironies of having to have a lion as her defender in iii 6–7.

At the end of Chapter 3, I raised some very large feminist issues in relation to the poem. There I suggested that you tried giving an account of the narrative of the first two cantos of the *Faerie Queene* from Una's point of view. This is a good moment, although it will itself involve a minor digression, to extend that exercise and the approach glanced at there. Do you think there are differences of interest and tone that mark the narratives of Redcrosse and Una as distinct? Does the text allow a difference between male and female narratives? Is either preferable in the values it implies?

DISCUSSION

We may register that Redcrosse behaves in a 'manly' and heroic way, but take a look at the fight between Redcrosse and Sansfoy over Duessa in ii 15–16. Isn't this male contest over a female prize rendered comic? Is the epic simile of them as butting rams heroic or only mock-heroic? Surely Redcrosse's quest soon changes from a truly heroic to an erotic one, that is, he pursues Duessa instead of the dragon. When he meets Duessa in ii 13 his story restarts again (false starts?) in a stanza which rewords the original start of the poem in i 4. At the House of Pride he again fights over Duessa – and a shield. And what do you make of the tone of the language used in the description of the fight between Satyrane and Sansfoy (vi 43–45). One of the poem's editors says that here Spenser deliberately 'exhausts the conventions of chivalric combat'.[2] Is Una's patient and constant quest in seeking her knight, whom she is eventually instrumental in rescuing, any less 'heroic' than most of Redcrosse's activities in the first half of Book I?

Indeed, we have to ask explicitly what might constitute 'heroism' in *Faerie Queene*, Book I. As an illuminating comparison consider the way the narrator of Milton's *Paradise Lost* talks about heroism just before he is about to tell us of the fall of man (IX 1–47). Here is part of that passage:

> Wars, hitherto the only argument
> Heroic deemed, chief mastery to dissect
> With long and tedious havoc fabled knights
> In battles feigned; the better fortitude
> Of patience and heroic martyrdom
> Unsung; or to describe races and games,
> Or tilting furniture, emblazoned shields,
> Impreses quaint, caparisons and steeds;
> Bases and tinsel trappings, gorgeous knights
> At joust and tournament; ...[3]

Look at the way that the language of chivalric conflict is rendered here – 'tilting furniture', 'impreses [heraldic devices] quaint' and the very Spenserian phrase 'tinsel trappings' (cf. the description of Duessa, ii 13.8). Milton prefers to sing of 'the better fortitude/Of patience and heroic martyrdom' than the wrath of Achilles in the *Iliad*, or of the 'tilting furniture, emblazoned shields' of chivalric romance. I do not think the issue in Spenser is as simple as a rejection of the values of chivalry and romance, but surely Redcrosse's 'chivalric' behaviour in Book I is called into question, and consequently what constitutes knightly virtue, and this is partly done through the counterpoint of the narrative of Una's 'heroic' virtue. There is nothing as explicit as the opening of *Paradise Lost*, Book IX, but in his compassionate intervention of iii 1–3 the poet makes Una the hero of an alternative epic which is now necessary to save the errant Redcrosse. He uses the same typical formulaic opening of an epic ('For fairest Vnaes sake, of whom I sing', iii 2.1) as that in the epic formulae of first stanza of the Proem to the whole poem (Proem 1.5). Una's sufferings surpass those of the wandering epic hero Odysseus (iii 21.5). Her often emphasized patient, slow progress (ii 8.1–2, iii 4.2) which we saw first in her opening portrait, is surely a virtue compared with Redcrosse's rashness: her feminine constancy and fidelity preferable to the knight's unstable and undiscriminating passions.

My own brief, but I hope relevant, digression leads back to Book I's own digressive ways. What I propose is beginning to emerge is the *relevance*, not the distraction, of digressions: that Book I is in fact constituted by them. 'Digression' (from Latin *digredi*, to go aside), so the dictionary tells me, can mean depart, depart from course or track, diverge from right path, transgress, deviate from subject in writing. All these meanings are relevant to both the first episode of the book (Error) and the narratives of Book I itself. Like the Wandering Wood, the narratives of Book I are 'so many pathes, so many turnings' (I i 10.8). I wrote earlier of digressions which slow down the narrative and impede arrival at its end. What if digressiveness is the necessary condition of Spenser's and the knight's narrative? If we can think of the narratives of Una and Redcrosse counterpointing and commenting on each other, we could try the same approach with other stories and digressions.

In a typical moment when narrative progress apparently halts, Redcrosse and Duessa, weary of the journey, rest in the shade, and we and they hear the frightening and pitiful story of Fradubio. **Can we see this narrative as a piece of 'counterpoint', and if so, of what? Are there parallels, differences and therefore implied comments on the main narrative from which this looks like a digression? Reread ii 28–45 now with this point in mind. What do you find?**

DISCUSSION

Fradubio's story is very close to Redcrosse's own at this point in Book I. On the face of it a digression, it actually reruns Redcrosse's story and retells his infidelity. The first line of ii 40 brings the stories of Fradubio and Redcrosse to the same point. Some of the common details are: a chance meeting with Duessa accompanied by a knight; and through magic the knight's lady is made to seem ugly and disgraceful and is rejected in favour of Duessa. We can see that if the stories continue to run in parallel, then Redcrosse is in great danger. Indeed, he too will be weakened and transformed by Duessa as Fradubio was. Redcrosse here hears a story which has acute relevance to him in the warning it might have offered if he had 'read' it with comprehension. He does not realize, to quote Horace again, 'this story is also about you'. The symmetries and asymmetries are intriguing. The symmetry of unnamed knight–Duessa–Fradubio (ii 35) and Sansfoy–Duessa–Redcrosse (ii 12–14) enforces the similarity of Redcrosse and Fradubio. The apparent symmetry of Fraelissa–Fradubio–Duessa and Una–Redcrosse–Duessa is true in that it again reinforces the similarity of Fradubio and Redcrosse, but there is surely dis-symmetry in any implication that Fraelissa is like Una. Isn't it the dissimilarities that are important here? I realize in trying to work out these parallels myself that I think that Spenser is being witty and ironical having the promiscuously inconstant Duessa as the 'constant' value in all these parallel relationships of characters.

I will leave you to investigate more fully the extraordinarily detailed way Fradubio's story recapitulates Redcrosse's story so far. Look out for the minuteness of paralleled details – for example, the garland promised to the fairer of Duessa and Fraelissa (ii 37.5) echoes the garland with which Redcrosse thought to crown Duessa (ii 30), implying his mistaken preference for her over the absent Una. You could also consider the ways in which what we learn of Fradubio might imply things about Redcrosse which the narrator of the poem has not explicitly told us.

We can move to consider other apparent digressions from the dominant narratives in Book I. To take the examples I mentioned on p. 50: **what relevance do you think the passages on Aesculapius and then the further digression on Hippolytus might have to what is happening in the House of Pride in I v? Or what relevance might the story of Satyrane have to the events of I vi? Look again at the text to refresh your memory of details.**

DISCUSSION

Cantos vii–ix are crowded with dramatic incidents and strong contrasts of triumph and failure: Redcrosse's enfeeblement, the nadir of his imprisonment and rescue; the zenith of Duessa's triumphant triple crowning and enthronement; and then her fall and exposure, the arrival of Arthur. They also contain figures relating stories to each other: the dwarf concisely recapitulates the story of Redcrosse so far (vii 26), Una recapitulates her history and that of Redcrosse to Arthur (vii 42ff), and Arthur tells Una his early history, including the account of his encounter with the Faery Queen herself in dream-vision (if this is what it was, ix 1–17).

An interesting and complex comparison is the one that suggests itself between the story that Arthur tells and the story of Redcrosse up to this point. **By the time we reach the end of Arthur's narration at ix 17, what do you see as the similarities and differences between these knights and their stories so far? What conclusions might we draw from such a comparison?**

DISCUSSION

One's first reaction is, I think, that Redcrosse and Arthur are quite different and opposite, especially at this moment when Arthur has told his story. Arthur's portrait (vii 29–36) represented him as shining, vital, richly armoured. He is successful in battle, faithful to the Faery Queen, attentive to Una. Redcrosse, having just emerged from darkness and the dungeon, is weak, foul-smelling, wasted (viii 38–41), all the consequences of infidelity, inconstancy, defeat and disgrace through his encounters with Duessa and Orgoglio. Arthur is the triumphant and royal victor over the giant and the witch, and has exposed the foulness of Duessa, whose apparent beauty seduced, enchanted and so enfeebled Redcrosse.

But there are similarities, too. The portraits of both knights conform to Book I's typical pattern: mounted, accompanied, armed and unnamed (Arthur is not eventually and 'truly' named by Una until ix 6.5). The attention given to Arthur's armed outside resembles that of Redcrosse's at the beginning of the poem. The origins and hence identities of both knights are obscure and have yet to be revealed to them (ix 5). On p. 52 I implicitly criticized Redcrosse because his 'quest soon changes from a truly heroic to an erotic one', but isn't Arthur's search for his mistress, the Faery Queen, an erotic quest from its inception? Arthur has a ravishing dream experience (what *does* happen in ix 13–15?) of a fair maiden who lies beside him and who makes 'louely blandishment' to him? What is the difference between this and the experiences of Redcrosse in Archimago's house? Aren't the experiences the same, in detail? I am sure you can find many more ways in which the presentation of Arthur and Redcrosse and their careers in Book I differ from but also curiously and perhaps disquietingly resemble each other. I say 'disquietingly', because such resemblances lead us to question the certainty of our discriminations between likeness and unlikeness in Book I. In Chapter 3 we saw how the False Una and Duessa falsely duplicated the real Una, but I suppose we prided ourselves on our ability to distinguish between them with a perception superior to that of Redcrosse, who failed to do so. The discriminations necessary to distinguish between Redcrosse's dream experience of the False

Una and Arthur's of the Faery Queen are more difficult to make
and even more problematical to justify. Such distinctions and
how they affect our reading of the poem are important. As a way
of approaching an answer, try a few exercises in distinguishing
not, now, between narratives but between minor figures in *Faerie
Queene*, Book I.

In the following pairs or sets of characters, try the by now familiar
exercise of comparing and contrasting, this time asking especially
'*How* can I tell these apart' and '*How* can I be sure of what the
poem means me to think of them?'
    Corceca (iii 13–23) and Celia (x 1–11)
    Malvenu (iv 6), Ignaro (viii 30ff) and Humiltá (x 5).
    Una (i 4–5) and Idlenesse (iv 18–20)
As before, reread these passages and make notes on your answers.

DISCUSSION

I think that it is moderately easy to be clear about these. Corceca
and Celia are both elderly mothers who spend a lot of time
in prayer and who 'run' houses stayed in by Una. Corceca is
blind, malicious, lives in darkness, and is wrinkled and grubby
from sitting in all those ashes three times a week. She is rather
reminiscent of Error in her liking for a dark and unpleasant
dwelling. She resists Una's entrance and reviles her as she leaves.
Celia, however, is graceful in manner and speech. *Her* prayers are
mixed with good deeds, and she welcomes Una's visitation. In
spite of, indeed *because* of deliberate similarities we can tell them
apart as unpleasant and pleasant elderly women, largely because
of their reactions to Una. I feel that I am meant to find Corceca
stupid and malicious and her devotions absurd: Celia is benevolent, eloquent and serene. Similarity reinforces the recognition of
difference.
        Malvenu ('Bad Welcome'), Ignaro and Humiltá are all porters.
The first, porter to the House of Pride, denies access to none. The
last, porter to the House of Holiness, keeps a carefully guarded
door. Ignaro, porter to Orgoglio's castle, does not even know how
to use the keys. The first is indiscriminate, the third cautious, and
Ignaro is just stupid.
        I am sure that you found numerous differences between
Idlenesse and Una, but also noticed that both ride an ass and both
are clothed in black. But perhaps you also noticed the distinction that Idlenesse rides a 'slouthfull Asse' (iv 18.7) and Una a
'lowly Asse'; and you recalled from Chapter 3 that Una's black

actually conceals an extraordinary whiteness. One could go on holding up pairs of figures for comparison in this way. You could try this exercise on Archimago (i 29–35) and Contemplation (x 46–49), and (although this may seem bizarre) Error and Charissa (x 30–33).

The asses in the last paragraph seem to me to raise interesting questions. In Chapter 3 I said that I thought we could transfer the humility of Una's ass as a property of its rider. But apparently one cannot always trust an ass to signify humility: in the case of Idlenesse it signifies its rider's sloth. Lions, too, can be ambiguous signs. Remember that for the bestiary writer they signify the risen Christ (see p. 28), but for the writer of the first Epistle of Peter a lion signifies the devil seeking to destroy mankind. Seen in this way, the ass and the lion are examples of the possible arbitrary relation of signs to significance. Allegorical 'language' might be usefully thought of in terms of some theories of the linguist Saussure. For him a linguistic sign is made up of a *signifier* (sounds, letters, marks or other inscriptions of meaning) and a *signified* (a conceptual meaning). For Saussure the relationship between signifier and signified is arbitrary and is based on agreed conventions and contexts rather than on a necessary and unchangeable link between them. So in the allegorical 'language' of the poem you are reading, the ass can signify humility *or* sloth. In a sharper paradox, as we have seen in the course of this *Guide*, the lion can in different contexts signify Christ *or* the devil. Constant care is apparently needed in reading signs in an allegorical language, for they can carry different senses.

Two last exercises in reading. Look at the description of the lady eventually named by the poem as Lucifera (iv 6–12). Think about the ways in which the poem asks you to look at her and shapes your response to her as a reader. Since Lucifera is 'a mayden Queene' I'd like you to think of her in comparison to the portrait of another royal figure in Book V, the queen Mercilla (V ix 27–33).

DISCUSSION

Lucifera's surroundings are splendid: 'glorious' 'sumptuous', 'noble' and 'fair'. The first and strongest impressions are of a great queen enthroned and shining down on us with a brilliant light. Stanzas 7–8 dazzle us and her court into admiration of her beauty and royalty. We are constantly craning our necks to look up at her. She is a royal maiden like Una and, as sixteenth-century

readers undoubtedly would have thought, Elizabeth I. Take a look
at some of the well-known and often reproduced formal portraits
of Elizabeth,[4] especially the 'Rainbow' portrait at Hatfield House
reproduced on the cover of your Penguin edition of the poem.
Like Una, whose last appearance in Book I is in a blaze of light
(xii 21–23), Lucifera is beautiful and shines like the sun. But as
we read on, we may register her pride, aspiration and vanity. The
dragon at her feet (10.4–5) is an ominous sign, as is her name
when we are finally told it (12.1). By this point and in retrospect
we might notice the excessive quality of some of this queen's
features. I have already compared Lucifera to Una: is she so
very different from Mercilla, another 'mayden Queene of high
renowne' (V viii 17)? The method of description is very close:
approach to the presence of a great queen enthroned on high
under a royal canopy. I am sure you found numerous parallels and
also significant differences of detail – for example, Mercilla has a
lion not a dragon at her feet. Mercilla is one of the poem's most
transparent contemporary references. As you may have guessed,
and Spenser's original readers certainly did guess, she is a representation, among other things, of Elizabeth I. How can we tell
Lucifera and Mercilla apart, and for that matter Lucifera from
Una or Elizabeth I? The poem uses the same language, signs and
effects to describe them, especially those whose significance we
might have thought as being stable and univocal: virginity, light,
royalty, beauty. With Corceca and Celia, I said that comparison
reinforced the recognition of difference, with Lucifera one might
say that, in the instances we have tried, comparison obliterates
difference. It is easy to say that Mercilla is a deliberately com-
plimentary likeness of Elizabeth. Some critics would say that
Lucifera is so like Elizabeth that the portrait must be a conscious
or unconscious critique of the queen. I don't think that there is an
easy solution to these specific questions or to the general issues
that are raised.

**Finally, what seems to me to be a most taxing exercise for readers
of the *Faerie Queene*. How do we read the signs in the portrait of
Fidelia (x 12–20), who is generally thought to be a personification
of faith? Isn't she an unlikely and intimidating figure for faith?**

DISCUSSION

Fidelia's picture in x 12–13 is rather like a Renaissance *emblem*, a
woodcut or engraving visually expressing some moral or pro-

verbial meaning. Some of the signs are those we would think appropriate in a representation of faith: dazzling light, white robes, a golden cup of wine and water which may suggest the communion chalice to us. This figure may again remind us of some descriptions of Una. But light was not reliable as a sign of spiritual virtue in the portrait of Lucifera: indeed, Fidelia's light could daze the beholder just as Lucifera's does. And *is* the cup a communion chalice, as I (rashly?) wrote a couple of sentences ago? The last golden cup we saw in Book I was flowing with death and despair and was in the hands of a witch (viii 14). The book, sealed with blood and containing 'dark' and difficult things, is an ominous sign, and the effect on readers of the serpent in the cup is made explicit: 'That horrour made to all, that did behold' (13.5). And surely, aren't serpents signs of evil in *Faerie Queene*, Book I, all the way from Error to the dragon, including the one at Lucifera's feet and Duessa's seven-headed monster? Fidelia seems an off-putting figure who dazes, horrifies and perplexes. Even her name is perilously close to 'Fidessa', the alias adopted by Duessa. Yet there is good reason, so readers of the poem over four centuries tell us, to think that she represents faith. The iconography (that is, a tradition of artistic symbols and how they are understood), which is deployed in Fidelia is intriguing.[5] The history of the symbol of the serpent in the chalice makes it likely that it is here, among other things, a symbol for Christ. When the Israelites were bitten by snakes in the wilderness they were healed homeopathically, for Moses 'made a serpent of brasse, and set it up for a signe: and when a serpent had bitten a man, then he looked to the serpent of brasse, and lived' (Numbers 21:9). And so, according to John 3:14, 'as Moses lift up the serpent in the wildernesse, so must the Sonne of man be lift up'. The Gospel verse appropriates the Old Testament image of the brazen serpent in an instance of intertextual and typological allegory of the kind we looked at on pp. 20–2. Now I do not think that there is any 'natural' way for readers to guess or infer that a serpent might represent Christ or that Fidelia's serpent signifies Christ, especially as he is present in the wine at communion. Yet I think that this is part of the point. Reading the allegory of Fidelia requires an act of faith which is analogous to the very concept which Fidelia in fact allegorically represents, and also to the act of faith required to believe that Christ is in some way present in the chalice at communion. We might have to have faith, I suppose ultimately in the system of signs or in its deviser (Spenser in the poem, God in the world), to read 'rightly' signs which perplex and challenge us with their contrariness and test us with their apparent arbitrariness. Remember that both the lion *and* the serpent can mean Christ *or* Satan (literally 'the adversary').

I have been asking you in this chapter of the *Guide* to work hard at reading extended and digressive narratives and at reading signs. Following the digressive narratives of Spenser's romance quests and reading signs along the journey can be taxing, for readers share in the same arduous experiences as the knights of Book I, even as they share in the experience of reading. The journey for us all is delightful, digressive and difficult. Entry into, experience in and exit from the Wandering Wood is the initiatory paradigm for many of the reading experiences of Book I. I would like to consider at the end of this chapter how the work of reading I have asked you to do, and the conclusions you may have reached about it, affect what I hope is a developing sense of what is involved in reading Spenser's allegorical poem.

From classical antiquity onwards thinking of all sorts (for example, argument, classification, ideas of virtue) has often been done in terms of contraries. Early Christianity continued this oppositional thinking: good and evil, heaven and hell, time and eternity. St Augustine said, in a formulation influential on later thought, that evil was nothing other than the privation of good, and he went on:

> That which is called evil, well ordered and positioned in its proper place, sets off good to greater advantage, as good is more pleasing and more praiseworthy when compared with evil.[6]

Ben Jonson thought that the duty of the poet was exactly this proper disposition and opposition of good and evil;

> We do not require in him mere elocution; or an excellent faculty in verse; but the exact knowledge of all virtues, and their contraries; with ability to render the one loved, the other hated, by his proper embattling them.[7]

In the Renaissance, thinking in terms of binary opposition (see p. 45) was a characteristic of the period's mentality and of its taste in rhetorical figures and we have seen the way that so many rhetorical figures are constituted by the play between the 'one' and the 'other'.

Truth, virtue and right reading seem defined in Book I by this same play of binary opposites that characterizes its pairing of figures, incidents and places and orders its counterpointed narratives. The knights of Book I, like the warrior of Ephesians, engage in a dualistic spiritual struggle against 'the princes of the darkenes of this worlde'. Milton, just before a famous passage in his *Areopagitica* (1644) in which he says that Spenser is a better teacher than the medieval theologians, claims that progress and testing in a fallen world are by struggle with contraries:

> Assuredly we bring not innocence into the world..., we bring impurity much rather: that which purifies us is trial, and trial is by what is contrary.

It is this same binary play which we have seen to constitute metaphor (which declares identity while assuming difference), and allegory (which, as Dante observed, comes from *alleon*, 'the other' – see p. 29), which can be seen as 'talking about something else' or as play between texts.

I think that all this may well have a bearing on the relation of the two main female figures in Book I, and as I write this I become aware that so many of the reading exercises I asked you to do in this chapter have been of pairs of female figures. A passage from a mid-sixteenth-century treatise on rhetoric seems to me to illustrate this exactly:

> By contraries set together, thynges oftentymes appere greater... sette a faire woman against a foule, and she shal seeme muche the fairer, and the other muche the fouler. Accordyng whereunto there is a saiyng in Logique *Contaria inter se opposita magis elucescunt*. That is to say, contraries beeying set, the one against the other, appere more evident.[8] Therefore if any one be disposed to set furthe [forth] chastitie, he may bryng in, of the contrarie parte, whoredome, and show what a foul offence it is to live so unclenly, and then the deformitie of whoredome shall muche sette forthe chastitie.[9]

You will find Spenser himself saying something similar in III ix 2. In this passage you can see these ideas about oppositional thought, antithesis in rhetorical figures and the binary representation of women, all acutely relevant to this chapter's investigation of Book I of the *Faerie Queene*.

To end this chapter I want now to take this idea of a play of contraries one step further, not so much in an attempt to end their play and, to paraphrase Augustine, to order and position them in their proper place, but to pursue the idea, at its most arresting in Fidelia, of examples of meanings which are exactly the opposite of the apparent signification of words.

In earlier thought, hand in hand with the idea of contrast as a means of clarification went the idea of truthful expression by saying exactly the opposite. Medieval mystics said that the most appropriate way of talking about divine things was in the most dissimilar terms we can imagine. In this way we might clearly recognize the impossibility of attempting to represent divine

things. In addition, the incongruity of what Saussure would call
signifier and signified makes the sign more arresting and stimulat-
ing, as I think is the intention in Spenser's Fidelia. Irony is a way
of speaking in which we regularly say one thing and mean the
opposite. Early theorists of rhetoric were interested in this idea of
the opposite in thought and expression. The Roman rhetorician,
Quintilian, says that we have to admit the remarkable fact that
the etymological derivation of certain words comes from their
opposites, pointing to the word for 'grove', *lucus*, called so
because *parum luceat*, 'it lacks light'. That is, he makes an
etymological and 'meaningful' connection between two ideas that
are opposite: dark and light.[10] Isidore uses Quintilian's example
when he talks about the rhetorical figure antiphrasis: 'Antiphrasis
is a discourse understood through its opposite, such as 'grove'
[*lucus*] which lacks light [*lucem*] because of the excessive shadiness
of its trees'. Antiphrasis, as the Renaissance writer on rhetoric
Peacham explained, is 'when a word is understoode by the
contrary, as we use commonly to say, this is wel done, when we
meane the contrary'.[11] Most pertinent to our puposes is Quintilian
on allegory. You are now accustomed to the idea that allegory, in
Quintilian's words, 'presents one thing in words and another in
meaning'. But then unnervingly the same sentence continues 'or
else something completely opposite to the meaning of the words'.[12]
Truth, then, may be constituted by distinguishing between contraries and with effort is distinguished especially clearly when
those contraries appear similar. But truth, as well as falsehood,
may also be expressed by saying the opposite.

Try, finally, to work out these passages of dizzying double
negatives in Book I. After Night has been put off by Duessa's
(false) light, Duessa protests her identity to Night. Look at the
play of false and true, of being and seeming in Duessa's statement,
'I that do seeme not I, *Duessa* am' (v 26.6). Try playing with the
punctuation, shifting around or adding commas to see how the
meanings are elusive and changing ('I, that do seeme not I, *Duessa*
am'; 'I that do seeme not, I *Duessa* am', etc.). Actually, isn't
Duessa (unwittingly?) made to speak the truth here through
doubleness and opposites? Whatever Duessa may say, one of the
few true facts about her in Book I emerges: that is she is not what
she seems. Night's final recognition of Duessa in the following
stanza (v 27.2–6) is also an example of the double play of false
and true:

> In that faire face
> The false resemblance of Deceipt, I wist

Did closely lurke; yet so true-seeming grace
It carried, that I scarse in darkesome place
Could it discerne

We might expect double-talk from Night and Duessa, but look also at the way that Una has to use language in telling Arthur about the wiles of Archimago which caused Redcrosse's defection:

all vnweeting, an Enchaunter bad
His sence abusd, and made him to misdeeme
My loyalty, not such as it did seeme (vii 49.3–5)

Doubleness is the necessary condition of allegory, as is digressiveness ('assuredly we bring not innocence into the world...'). As well as all the other things that allegory may be, it is what A. Bartlett Giamatti calls, in the title (borrowed from *Faerie Queene*, Book III) of an excellent short book which I would recommend to you, the 'play of double senses'.[13]

5. Temperate Reading

'So entirely are beauty and delight in it the native element of Spenser, that, whenever in *The Faerie Queene* you come suddenly on the moral, it gives you a shock of unpleasant surprise, a kind of grit, as when one's teeth close on a bit of gravel in a dish of strawberries and cream'

(James Russell Lowell, 'Spenser' 1875[1])

In the course of guiding you through Book I of the *Faerie Queene*, I have asked you to move from small-scale and particular readings in Chapters 1 and 2 to a consideration of the large structuring patterns of Book I. At the same time, I have asked you to consider some general critical approaches to Spenser's poem and also some material on allegorical reading. Here I want to open up a discussion of Book II, then in Chapter 6 proceed to a more particular examination. In both chapters I want you to keep in mind the highly self-conscious activity of reading allegory, and the allegorical practices of Spenser's contemporaries and predecessors that we have looked at already.

Let's start with the most general impressions. **Read Book II, making notes on its narrative structure, its major events, figures and locations. How does it compare with Book I for its power to engage your interest as a reader? Is it like Book I in its scale and scope and pace? Are there any differences?**

DISCUSSION

After Book I, many readers, especially new readers, of Book II of the *Faerie Queene* often experience disappointment. Some even find large parts of it boring and slow. C. S. Lewis registered the impression, although he thought it a mistaken one, that after Book I the rest of the *Faerie Queene* sinks away to book VI.[2] The events of Book II certainly seem less exciting. In Book I the legend of Holiness told of the highly coloured career of Redcrosse: foolishly deceived, seduced by a witch, imprisoned by a giant, tempted to despair and finally triumphantly recovering and killing a dragon in an epic three-day battle. This is followed, in Book II, by the slower-moving legend of Temperance: Guyon's attempts to pacify some irascible figures, his tying up an old woman (II iv), his trip in a gondola trying to be polite to the empty-headed Phaedria (II vi), his underground trip at the end of which he faints (II vii). Contrasted with large dramatic pictures of Book I (think of Duessa triumphant on her beast or Redcrosse fighting the dragon), the scenes here are more like miniatures, some of them almost comically grotesque: Amavia with the little baby playing in her blood (II i–ii), Furor dragging along Phedon by his hair (II iv 3), Braggadocchio hiding from Belphoebe in a bush (II iii 21). Book I's dualistic conflicts of truth and falsehood, light and dark were dramatic and on a large scale, and informed its structure, incidents and images in certain ways, as we have seen. Book II's range of expression seems different and quieter. The disappointment of readers may be because they are not getting more of the sort of thing thay had become used to and had come to enjoy in Book I.

Let us try and be more specific about the different scope, pace and tone of Book II. Is your interest in its events of the same kind as in Book I? Is its narrative as exciting?

DISCUSSION

There are obvious anticlimaxes in the events, as in the encounters with Furor (II iv) and Pyrochles (II v), where Guyon stops short of the final violent exertion we expect necessary to lead to victory. And doesn't the encounter with Mammon end inconclusively, even bathetically, in Guyon's faint, which makes him vulnerable to the combined forces of Pyrochles, Cymochles, Atin and Archimago at the beginning of II viii? Isn't the end of the whole book anticlimactic? Instead of Redcrosse's triumph over the dragon and final betrothal to Una, Guyon walks (increasingly slowly) through a garden. In II xi it is Arthur who does the fighting.

If you have the same experience as me of Book II, why does the tone at times seem so sober and even bleak, and why does the experience of reading through it seem more arduous than that of reading Book I? What replaces the narrative excitement of Book I?

DISCUSSION

The tone of Book II is sober and marked by sententious pronouncements on life, often on mortality. There seems an awareness of what is wrong with human life and disturbs it: irrational swings of emotion in its characters, the nightmarish ailments that assault the castle of Alma (II xi). There is a great sense of the frailty and vulnerable physicality of human life and happiness right from Amavia's tragedy at the beginning. Guyon faints through exhaustion and lack of food and water after his trials in the House of Mammon, and the best of knights is assaulted by both impotence and impatience (xi 23ff). The Palmer and Guyon are given to bleak aphorisms and meditations on life. When Amavia dies Guyon points her and her tragic story out to the Palmer and us as an example – 'Behold the image of mortalitie' (i 57.2) – and for him Amavia's child is an image of the miserable state of man (ii 2). But 'So feeble is mans state, and life vnsound' (xi 30.3) and 'no earthly thing is sure' (ix 21.9) are comments of the *poet*, not of one of his fictional figures, and suggest a more austere tone for the whole book.

For these reasons the narrative is less colourful and exciting than in Book I, and the whole book is more static, because in place of narrative we have many lengthy descriptive or discursive passages. If we experienced interruptions in Book I's narrative as digressions, aren't the interruptions in Book II more descriptive and pictorial? For example, there is the extended portrait of Belphoebe at II iii 21–31. She does not appear again in this book, but we get here the most elaborate portrait in the poem: it is substantially longer than Arthur's at I vii 29–36. And I would be surprised (and impressed by your thorough patience as readers) if you had read every word of the history of British and Elfin kings in II x. Few readers come away from the chronicles in this canto like Arthur and Guyon, 'Beguild thus with delight of nouelties' (II x 77). There are long descriptions, too, of locations: Alma's Castle in II ix; and the 87 stanzas containing the Bower of Bliss make II xii the longest canto in the entire poem. In the Bower of Bliss, Book II is at its most static and most descriptively pictorial.

Also, doesn't debate often replace action in Book II? In Book I Redcrosse's debate with despair is an untypical moment. By contrast, there is a quantity of debate, discussion and argument in Book II: between Guyon and the Palmer, Guyon and Mammon, Guyon and Arthur. One can see why all this debate seems to have made it Milton's favourite book of the *Faerie Queene*. There is also much discourse and exposition: the workings of the human body and mind allegorically represented in the House of Alma, and British 'history' in the chronicles Arthur and Guyon read there.

And what do we make of Guyon, the knight of Temperance? If he embodies or is moving towards the virtue of the book, does the presentation of Guyon make us desire the virtue he represents? Or to put it more crudely, do we *like* Spenser's Guyon? **Reread, for example, vi 19–38. I hope that you will agree that this is not an untypical example.**

DISCUSSION

Some readers have thought that Guyon fails in his quest, fails to embody temperance, and thus fails to convince us of his ability to exercise it and hence of its desirability as a virtue. These criticisms focus particularly on his behaviour in the book's last canto, to which I will return in the next chapter. More generally, readers have found Book II's protagonist less appealing than the Redcrosse knight. Offered a choice between Redcrosse's failures and Guyon's successes, which do you find more engaging: the fallible knight of holiness, or the often icy composure of the virtuous Guyon? Guyon treats figures who are victims of their passions with unendearing sternness. Indeed, of all the heroes in the poem Guyon has provoked the most extreme critical disagreement. Surely he often appears in awkward or embarassing predicaments?

There is the shaming necessity of Guyon's having to fight with an old woman (as Atin points out at iv 45.2−5). This struggle anticipates the violence done to Acrasia in II xii: Guyon's quest is achieved, embarassingly, not in killing a monster, but in chaining up a beautiful woman and then trashing her garden. Some readers have found that Guyon is upstaged by other events in Book II. Some have found him insipid, or worse still, and especially in II xii, a killjoy. They have found him at the end of Book II, like one of his literary descendants, the Lady in Milton's *Comus*, a sententious 'self-righteous prig', or alternatively a repressed neurotic. Of all Spenser's protagonist knights Guyon is not a lover or in search of love (or does his blushing courting of Shamefastnesse at ix 40−44 faintly count?).

One way of thinking of Guyon which I have found useful, in company with some other readers, is to imagine him as very young, even late adolescent. The first description of Guyon (i 6) gives little away on which to base what may be a flight of interpretative fancy: comely, upright, demure, temperate (of course), stern and terrible. I suppose I am assuming that Guyon looks rather like his guardian angel (viii 5.1−4), and that he resembles Verdant in whom, frighteningly, he sees a possible image of what he could become (xii 79−81). Might thinking of Guyon as very young be a way of accounting for his awkwardnesses, his rigorous views, even his hysterical reaction to Acrasia? You may find this approach unfair to both Guyon and late adolescents; it may also strike you as critically dangerous, as it may encourage us to think of such Spenserian figures as Guyon as being of the same kind as as those in nineteenth-century novels or early twentieth-century plays which attempt to give us the illusion of 'real' people. On the other hand, it may be a useful shorthand for thinking about the way that Spenser has chosen to present this particular knight and the quality he represents and exercises. Book I's analysis was of man's spiritual state, its discourse religious and theological: remember the display of personified vices in the House of Lucifera and the virtues and spiritual states personified in the House of Celia. Isn't it the case that we could think of Book II as more concerned with man's emotions, with what we would now call the representation of psychology? After all, the workings of the mind and its relationship to the body are anatomized by the allegory of the House of Alma and the battle to defend it (II ix and II xi).

I realize that I have been putting a sort of devil's advocate's case against Book II, and latterly against Guyon himself, and even then going to the extent of implicitly excusing him on the grounds of a sort of immaturity. But a case against Book II is not just a rhetorical ploy at this point in this *Guide*, for I have to confess to the not untypical experience of finding parts of Book II arduous to read. I come away from the legend of Temperance with an uneasy impression that I might have read it with satisfaction almost in spite of itself. But let us at least consider that Book II represents what Spenser intended and start from his own title, 'The Legend of Sir Guyon, or of Temperance'. Temperance is a word and a concept (and sometimes a practice) that is unfamiliar to us. If it calls any associations at all to mind, I suppose the most likely is 'temperance hotels' where one is not allowed to drink alcohol. As temperance is certainly a more unfamiliar idea than holiness, which was the legend of Book I, I want to investigate briefly the *semantic field* of 'temperance', that is, the area of related meanings in and around the word. **If you have access to a good dictionary you could look up 'temperance' together with some of its *cognate* (related) words, especially 'temper' (as a noun and a verb) and 'temperament'. You could also look up other words in this field such as 'temperate'.**

DISCUSSION

Here is a brief account of the information my dictionaries yielded. The verb 'temper' comes from the Latin verb *temperare*, to divide, or to mingle or combine in proper proportion. So, by extension, it can apparently mean such things as modify, mingle, and so persuade, appease, regulate, restrain, guide, tune, bring to harmony, even restore to health.

So the noun 'temper' used to mean a proportionate mixture or condition, a bodily or mental constitution, and hence such things as middle course, balance, moderation. We now chiefly think of 'temper' as 'anger', as when we are 'in a temper'. The more old-fashioned 'to be *out of* temper' is closer to its original meanings, that is, being angry is being out of balance or condition and disturbs an equable 'temper' or 'temperament'. 'Temperament' embodies these ideas of a moderate and proportionate mixture, and is a middle course between extremes: 'temperamental' (erratic, liable to moods), like 'in a temper' is a modern usage where the meaning has been more or less reversed. And 'temperance' is therefore self-restraint, moderation, especially moderation in the pursuit of gratifying pleasure: it is an avoidance of excess, a mingling and combining.

How might we apply the sense we now have about the semantic field of 'temperance' to *Faerie Queene*, Book II? Does it help to account at all for the different and particular feeling of this book as I have been describing it?

Looking back to p. 64, I see that 'disappointing', 'rather boring', 'less exciting' are the reactions I have imputed to at least some of you as readers of *Faerie Queene*, Book II, based partly on my own reactions to this book and also on those of other readers I have talked to. I also described it as seeming on a smaller scale. Perhaps this is a case of misrepresenting a reaction by using loaded and unfair words. If temperance involves notions of restraint, balance and moderation, might not sobriety and reserve in action and tone in Book II be appropriate and intended? If moderation is implicit in the ideas of temperance, might not Book II 'moderate' the effects of Book I? I suggested in Chapter 4 (pp. 50–3) that the counterpointing of the narratives of Una and Redcrosse in Book I calls into question what constitutes knightly virtue. So Book II might call for a different mixture of qualities in its particular ideal and expression of heroism. Earlier I described the encounter with Furor as anticlimactic. **Bearing in mind the field of meanings you have built up for 'temperance', try thinking about the *virtues* of the scene with Phedon, Furor and Occasion (II iv) as an expression of temperance in content and in style. Reread iv 1–16.**

DISCUSSION

The scene opens in noise, violence and madness (iv 3) and continues (4–5) with the grotesque emblematic (see Chapter 4, pp. 48–9) picture of Occasion. Guyon's reaction, even before he has seen anything, is to wish 'to agree' (conciliate, iv 3.4) whatever the disturbance is. Guyon's attempts at restraining Furor are met with biting, kicking and scratching (6). In wrestling with Furor Guyon 'ouerthrew himselfe' (8.9), got pummelled in the face, and, his heart 'emboyling', drew his sword. At this point the Palmer intervenes and directs both Guyon and the reader about *this* book's way of dealing with its virtue's opponents (II iv 10.2–5):

> Not so, ô *Guyon*, neuer thinke that so
> That Monster can be maistred or destroyd:
> He is not, ah, he is not such a foe
> As steele can wound, or strength can ouerthroe.

Contrast the stark alternatives and the antithesis in expression in Una's advice about fighting Error 'Strangle her, else she sure will strangle thee' (I i 19.4). Look at the verbs in the Palmer's advice about handling Furor and Occasion (II iv 11): tame, amenage [control], restraine, withstood, asswage, calme, stopped. They come from the semantic field of the verb 'temper'. Even 'is withdrawen', although it looks like an action on the part of Occasion, can also mean 'restrained', that is, by a regulating agent whose activity is so moderate that it can grammatically seem like the action of the object of control. The Palmer's considered and balanced advice is also very different from Una's urgent shout 'Add faith vnto your force' (I i 19.3). There is certainly a sense of Milton's struggle with and trial by contraries here, but the answer is not simply dramatic and aggressive opposition. It is an important moment in Book II, for the encounter with Furor is in many senses Guyon's 'first emprise' (enterprise, undertaking, II iv 12.1) and a moment in which we might expect his virtue and its expression beginning to form themselves.

You will find another *avoidance* of battle when at the beginning of the book (II i 26ff) Guyon and Arthur draw back in time from conflict with each other. Look at the symmetry and restraint in the carefully balanced and parallel addresses (mutual apologies and polite self-deprecation in 27–28) and actions (both lift their helmets and greet each other, 'Goodly comportance each to other beare', 29.3).

So persuasion, appeasement, regulation, restraint and self-restraint, all in the semantic field of 'temper' and 'temperance', are likely to be features of both Guyon's heroism and the poetic style of Book II. Look at the ways that Guyon deals with Pyrochles in II v and see if you think this episode also articulates these qualities. And doesn't the extended struggle in the House of Mammon consist in self-restraint, and victory is achieved by Guyon's making a virtue of constant negative but courteous and moderate response to Mammon's offers? The mode is extended debate rather than exciting physical conflict. I am not sure, however, whether this goes any way towards ameliorating my sense as a reader of the *arduousness* of II vii.

And then there is the sense in which temperance means health, a balanced bodily or mental constitution. **Where do you see these meanings at play in Book II? Look especially at cantos ix and xi.**

DISCUSSION

Most obviously, of course, in the House of Alma (ix) which gives us an anatomy of the workings of the temperate body and mind, and in Arthur's fight with distempered assaults on the body. 'Temperance' as a healthy constitution explains the medical discourse of cantos ix and xi. But notice also the way that Guyon's vital powers are weakened for want of food and sleep in the House of Mammon. I wonder if, as some readers have done, we are to see his weakness and faint as proceeding from an excessive self-testing (or self-reliance) which intemperately has stretched his physical resources too far?

I think that further investigation of both the incidents and the style of Book II in terms of the field of meanings around 'temperance' will yield illuminating results, and will leave you to do this work. For example, look at those figures 'out of temper', that is, wrathful, in II i–vi, or at the temperateness of disposition and description which govern Belphoebe's beauty (II iii 21–31).

I would like now to concentrate on a very particular knot of ideas concerning 'temperance' – the middle way, balance, moderation, the middle course between extremes, avoidance of excess. In Chapter 1 (p. 61) I cited Aristotle's *Rhetoric* on figurative language, and in Chapter 2 (p. 30) his *Poetics* on metaphor in particular. Aristotle's works strongly influenced all branches of European thought, especially from the twelfth century onwards, and he was the most widely read classical author in the Renaissance. His writings on moral philosophy had permeated Renaissance thought, especially those in his *Ethics* which was particularly respected by Protestant educators. For example, the Tudor educationalist, Sir Thomas Elyot, thought that by the age of 17 a young man was ready for the first two books of the *Nicomachean Ethics*.[3] One way Aristotle recommends thinking of virtue or goodness is in terms of moderation, the middle way or 'mean', a noun whose significances in a dictionary you would find interesting to compare with the work you have done on 'temper'. Here is part of a passage where Aristotle sums up his argument. Can you see how versions of this idea of a virtuous and 'temperate' mean are articulated in *Faerie Queene*, Book II? Note also Aristotle's quotation from the *Odyssey* at the end. We will come back to this in the next chapter.

> That moral virtue is a mean, then, and in what sense it is so, and that it is a mean between two vices, the one involving excess, the other deficiency, and that it is such because its character is to aim at what is intermediate in passions and in actions, has been sufficiently stated. Hence also it is no easy task to be good. For in everything it is no easy task to find the middle, e.g. to find the middle of a circle is not for everyone but for him who knows; so, too, anyone can get angry – that is easy – or give or spend money; but to do this to the right person, to the right extent, at the right time, with the right motive, and in the right way, *that* is not for everyone, nor is it easy; wherefore goodness is both rare and laudable and noble.
>
> Hence he who aims at the intermediate must first depart from

what is the more contrary to it, as Calypso advises –
    Keep the craft away from the smoke and breakers [*Odyssey*, XII
219–20][4]

I am struck by how Aristotle's illustrations and even his
asides provide an apt commentary on individual moments in
Spenser's legend of temperance. The proper use of money is ex-
plored in the House of Mammon (II vii), where Guyon is repeatedly
and meticulously careful and moderate in his replies to Mammon's
offers of wealth. Aristotle's notion of virtue as scrupulous behaviour taking into consideration exactly the right person, extent,
time, and motive brings to mind the precise care with which
Guyon behaves in very tricky situations when exactly the right
behaviour is difficult. Look, for example, at the way he deals
scrupulously with the tediously empty-headed and prattling
Phaedria in II vi. And the sense I get from Aristotle of the difficulty of virtue ('Hence also it is no easy task to be good')
corresponds with my experience as a reader of the inner arduousness of Guyon's exercise of virtue, even the constant *strain* he
experiences in the House of Mammon and I experience in reading
II vii.

The central point here is Aristotle's notion of 'a mean'. He
says that virtue aims at the middle, avoiding excess on the one
hand, deficiency on the other. Sobriety, stasis, debate, composure
are words I have been using about Book II and are all words
which might be seen as seeking a middle way. You will find that
the Palmer incorporates measuring out the mean and being in
the middle into his idea of temperance in i 58. We have already
seen ways in which Guyon attempts to achieve or maintain
equilibrium. The pattern of a middle as a sort of fulcrum balanc-
ing opposites is most obvious in Medina's castle. **Can you see how
the mean informs the narrative and images here (ii 12–46)?**

DISCUSSION

It is difficult to miss the pattern of the 'mean' in this canto.
Medina is one of three sisters who attempts to reconcile her
warring and quite different siblings who also quarrel with her, 'the
middest' (13.9). Look at the symmetrical patterning of stanzas
34–36 which describes the sisters: ironically poetic symmetry
'tempers' (in the sense of regulates) their unruliness. Look also at
the description of Medina (14–15) for another example of a
'restrained' style. In fact you may find the exemplification of the
mean in this episode rather relentless in its symmetries and the
constant pattern of the middle trying to balance two extremes.

It is repeated in the symmetrical but radically opposed and temperamental suitors of Elissa and Perissa, thus implying Guyon as their balanced temperate 'mean'. It even characterizes the epic simile in stanza 24. Look out for the mean as a pattern of three with one in the middle as the one which tends to control groupings of figures in this book, sometimes ironically: Mortdant, Ruddymaine and Amavia (i); Furor, Phedon and Occasion (iv) are two examples. Maleger is attended by two hags, Impatience and Impotence, in a parody of the temperate mean (xi).

'Rather relentless' in the last paragraph as a description of the poetry's exemplification of the mean raises again that doubt about Book II. We can see what the poetry is doing with notions of temperateness, but are we sufficiently held and satisfied by it? Such doubts about this canto were expressed by C. S. Lewis, one of this century's most eloquent champions of Spenser: 'Aristotle's doctrine of the Mean is (rather dully) allegorized' in II ii.[5] We must readdress this question again about Book II, particularly in relation to its last long canto, which has for a long time raised not only this particular question but also crucial questions about reading Spenser's poetry and indeed the poetry of the Renaissance in general. We will consider all these issues in the next chapter.

Finally in this chapter, since I have been entertaining the idea that Book II of the *Faerie Queene* might suffer by comparison with Book I, I would like you to consider the relations of the two books and the relation of their allegories more generally.

Spenser's allegory proceeds in geometric rather than arithmetical progression. In previous chapters and in reading Book I, we have seen the play of meanings within an allegorical field in one book. We saw how allegorical meanings were produced, for example, by paired descriptions of women, by images of light and dark, by the repeated motif of the serpent. This production of meaning took place, as it were, horizontally, so we saw in Chapter 4 that meaning in Book I was constituted by binary play within the same book. As our reading of each successive book of the poem is added to the previous ones, there will be an increasing vertical dimension to play within Spenser's allegorical poem. To use an image not entirely unrelated to criticism of Book II, you might think of Spenser's poem as a particularly rich cake consisting of alternate layers of pastry, chocolate, cream, strawberries, nuts or whatever happens to be your taste in rich cakes. Each layer is constituted by its particular ingredients. To make the cake these layers are then piled up, and when a slice is taken out for us to eat we can see in that slice the layers of nuts, cream and so on. In an extremely rich cake we can see, say, repeated layers of strawberries or two layers like coffee and chocolate which have some of the same ingredients but are not identical. So in reading more of the *Faerie Queene* we will have an accumulating sense of a 'vertical' interrelation between the fields of play of the successive books. To get a simple sense of how this works try some examples of the exercises in Chapter 4. In Chapter 4 I asked how we could tell apart Lucifera, Mercilla, Una and Elizabeth I. **How are Lucifera and Mercilla like, and to be distinguished from, Philotime (II vii 43ff)?**

DISCUSSION

Philotime has the same magnificent, overawing and royal setting as Lucifera and Mercilla. Guyon, eager courtiers and we approach the presence of another female prince shining in glory. The poem offers us the favour of this monarch as sought after and the way to advancement. Perhaps a subtle sense of oppressive weight ('vpbeare', 'massy', 'huge', 'sustayne', 43.5–6) distinguishes the mood of this scene from the dazzling light and height of Lucifera. In contrast to the heavy materiality of Philotime's royal surroundings, Mercilla's stateliness is refined towards the heavenly: her royal canopy is a cloud and she is attended by angels (V ix 28). A noisy crowd presses around Philotime (II vii 44): Order keeps the same crowd making 'troublous din' outside Mercilla's presence (V ix 23). Her throne is attended by personifications of prayers, kinds of justice and temperance. And Philotime's beauty is made, 'counterfeited': secretly she is criminal (II vii 45). It is possible, then, to keep distinguishing between such figures and now the additional experience of reading Philotime makes some distinctions and issues clearer. Lucifera provides us with a comparison for Philotime, but Philotime also causes us to reread Lucifera. Both are clarified by the comparison: Philotime at this moment in Book II, Lucifera in retrospect. As we read Philotime we reread Lucifera: the 'shady' materiality of Philotime's wealth is pointed up by and also points up Lucifera's dazzlingly self-absorbed vanity. But in Chapter 4 I said that some readers had suggested that Lucifera is a conscious or unconscious critique of Elizabeth I. Philotime is another princess whose favour is to be courted and who is surrounded by the same milling ambitious crowd we saw surrounding Lucifera. **Do you think this scene in Book II might be additional evidence for the poet's criticism of the ambitions of Elizabethan court life, and hence even of a princess whose favour is so fervently sought? You might consider other examples of such readings and rereadings: what, for example, does a comparison** of Guyon's encounter with Amavia (II i–ii) with Redcrosse's encounter with Fradubio (I ii) tell us?

DISCUSSION

At a similar point in the two books the knightly protagonist hears a terrible tale, one from a male narrator, the other from a female. Amavia's story of disaster caused by a witch parallels Fradubio's, and so implicitly sets up a comparison between Duessa and Acrasia, both of whom possess a magic cup. Both are tales of infidelity, one caused by misperception, the other by desire for pleasure. Both tales are admonitory ones. Redcrosse is unable to extract the moral from the one he hears, whereas Guyon actually articulates the moral of Amavia's. I am sure that other similarities and differences occurred to you. They point up not only the difference between the tellers of these tales but also their hearers and the different emphases of the two books of the *Faerie Queene* in which they are told.

Spenser's poem asks for an increasingly sophisticated reading of allegory as it progresses. As well as the multiple writings which, in Barthes' formulation (see p. 26), are focused on the reader of any one particular book of the *Faerie Queene*, the reading of each successive book will bring incidents and figures, and indeed the larger structure of cantos and whole books, into Barthes' 'mutual relations of dialogue, parody, contestation'.

This makes Spenser's poem particularly open to *reader-response theory*, which focuses on the way literary works are received by the reader and the contribution to the text's meaning that the reader makes in reading. Terry Eagleton's description of the assumptions of *reception theory*, which is very like reader-response theory, both concisely describes these theories of reading and also provides a neat summary of the position we are already taking up as readers of Spenser's allegorical poem and of allegory, after reading two books of the *Faerie Queene*:

> Reading is not a straightforward linear movement, a merely cumulative affair: our initial speculations generate a frame of reference within which to interpret what comes next, but what comes next may retrospectively transform our original understanding, highlighting some features of it and backgrounding others. As we read on we shed assumptions, revise beliefs, make more and more complex inferences and anticipations; each sentence opens up a horizon which is confirmed, challenged or undermined by the next. We read backwards, and forwards simultaneously, predicting and recollecting, perhaps aware of other possible realizations of the text which

our reading has negated. Moreover all of this complicated activity is carried out on many levels at once,...[6]

Book I was preoccupied with religious topics, with the theological virtue of holiness, the attaining of spiritual wholeness; Book II is concerned with the moral life and the virtue of temperance. If we were to use the technicalities of Dante's discussion of traditional exegesis (pp. 29, 33), we could say that Book II foregrounds 'the moral sense' of allegory. Theological reference and context are not excluded, rather they are presupposed and provided by Book I which began, you will remember, with insistent attention to close reading of 'Scripture' and of two figures with analogues in the Epistles. Book II builds on Book I. If we were in danger of forgetting, Spenser has an angel intervene to look after Guyon in his faint after three days in the House of Mammon which is the most obvious Scriptural imitation in Book II, as it imitates Christ's triple temptation in the wilderness. The forty days and nights in the wilderness are precisely replicated, one critic has argued, in the forty stanzas Guyon spends in Mammon's House (vii 26.5–66.4). This is an example of the critical attention that has been paid to significant numerological patterning by Spenser.

Book I was concerned with the representation of truth and falsehood. Book II deals with the governing of human nature and particularly with what we would now call the emotions and Spenser's contemporaries would have called the body and its faculties. Book II's 'temper' (the mixture that makes it up, its constitution), is different. The second half of Book II gives particular attention to appetites and the regulation of pleasure and in its last canto especially the regulation of pleasure in fiction, and it is particularly to that last canto of Book II that I want us now to turn.

6. Reading for Pleasure

'No sooner has a word been said, somewhere, about the pleasure of the text, than two policemen are ready to jump on you . . .'
(Roland Barthes, 'The Pleasure of the Text' in *Barthes: Selected Writings*, ed. Susan Sontag 1983, p. 411)

As I shall be asking you to look closely at the last canto of Book II, please reread it now. Given the extraordinary length of this canto, its numerous incidents and the great concentration of vivid pictures, it will be a good idea to adopt the same practice as when reading individual books of the *Faerie Queene*, that is, to make detailed notes or diagrams, perhaps even a map, for this canto.

I suggested at the end of Chapter 2 that you might find it illuminating for *Faerie Queene*, Book I, to read the Book of Revelation from the Bible. **It would be a good idea to read, in conjunction with II xii, at least part of the story of the Greek hero Odysseus: his encounters with Circe and then with the Sirens, and with Scylla and Charybdis, which you will find in the *Odyssey*, Books X and XII.** There are a number of modern translations available in paperback; Walter Shewring's is good.[1] You will find Ovid's retelling of these stories in *Metamorphoses*, Books XIII–XIV. In the meantime here's a brief précis of the significant events in *Odyssey*, Books X and XII.

In Book X of the *Odyssey*, Odysseus and his crew arrive by sea at Aeaea, the island home of Circe, a goddess with strange powers. A scouting party sent by Odysseus comes to Circe's house where they hear her singing with her beautiful voice and where wild animals fawn tamely on them. Circe welcomes them, but gives them a mixed potion which magically transforms them into pigs. Odysseus goes in search of them and is warned and advised

by a god, 'golden-wanded Hermes'. Protected by a magical plant,
Odysseus drinks without ill effects Circe's magic cup, where good
things are mingled with drugs. He overcomes Circe and accepts
on his terms her offer of sex. She eventually proves hospitable
and retransforms his men, so that they are more handsome than
before. She gives Odysseus good advice about the perils still to
face him in his sea journey, including a warning about the be-
witching Sirens who lure men to destruction with their 'honey-
sweet music'. She also warns him about the female monster,
Scylla, and the whirlpool, Charybdis, between which he must sail.
He successfully negotiates this middle passage in Book XII.

When you read *Faerie Queene*, II xii and make notes or diagrams
to keep track of notable places and happenings in it, note also
those incidents and motifs which remind you of these.

First, can you see which parts of the story of Odysseus have
been imitated or reworked in the incidents, characters and motifs
of II xii? It would be useful to look first at whatever account or
map of II xii you have and check off the Homeric antecedents.
What are the most obvious changes or elaborations in Spenser's
version?

Like Odysseus, Guyon with the Palmer and boatman are
making one of the sea voyages in Book II. In an epic simile in
vii 1, Guyon has already been compared to a ship's pilot in
dangerous seas. But Spenser in II xii has reordered the sequence of
events in the *Odyssey*. The episodes of the Gulf of Greediness and
Rock of Vile Reproach (1–9) and the quicksand, whirlpool
and monsters (18–26) rework Odysseus's encounter with Scylla
and Charybdis in *Odyssey*, Book XII. The appeals of Phaedria, the
lamenting maiden and the mermaids refashion the invitations of
Homer's Sirens. Spenser has reversed Homer's order of Sirens,
then Scylla and Charybdis. The end of II xii consists of a series
of incidents and pictures based on Odysseus's encounters with
the goddess and enchantress Circe. This again reverses Homer's
sequence which has Circe earlier in Book X. It looks as though
Spenser wanted his version of the Circe story as the climax of
Book II. And his imitation of the events on the isle of Aeaea
is complex. Guyon repeats Odysseus's encounter with an enchantress who transforms men into animals, but Odysseus eventually accepts Circe's sexual offer although on his own terms.
Guyon refuses the more diffused erotic invitations of Acrasia's
garden and reacts repressively and finally with violence to the
sight of Acrasia and Verdant (76–83). There is no compromise
with Spenser's Acrasia as there was with Homer's Circe, who
eventually proved helpful and hospitable. And there is more than

one imitation of the figure of Circe: look at the Circean features of Genius (46–49) and Excess (54–57). I must leave you to investigate further and think about other aspects of Spenser's imitation of Homer's story. What is the relation, for example, between the god Hermes and the Palmer? How are the animals retransformed in Homer and in Spenser? I would like you to think now about allegorization of Homer's story.

In Chapter 5 (pp. 71–2) we looked at a passage from Aristotle's *Ethics* which ended with a quotation from the *Odyssey*. Please go back and read this passage again, noting Aristotle's quotation from the *Odyssey* at the end. Look at the context in *Odyssey*, Book XII, from which he extracts the quotation, 'Keep the craft away from the smoke and breakers'. Bearing in mind its context in this passage, how do you think Aristotle is using the allusion, and for what puposes? (Do not worry for the moment about the mistake Aristotle makes in saying 'as Calypso advises...').

We have seen in this passage the way Aristotle defines virtue as the mean between vicious extremes of excess and deficiency, and in Chapter 5 looked at the way this idea was articulated in moments of *Faerie Queene*, Book II. Aristotle illustrates this idea of the mean by quoting Odysseus's instructions to his steersman about the best method of negotiating the dangerous passage between Scylla and Charybdis.

> Hence he who aims at the intermediate must first depart from what is the more contrary to it, as Calypso advises –
>   Keep the craft away from the smoke and breakers [*Odyssey*, XII 219–20, tr Shewring]

What we can see in Aristotle's quotation of Homer here is an allegorical reading of Homer. Odysseus's resolution to steer between the opposed monstrous dangers of Scylla and Charybdis is interpreted as the virtuous man's attempt to keep a moderate middle course and avoid excess. By implication, Odysseus sailing between monster and whirlpool is the moderate and virtuous man, Scylla and Charybdis the dangerous extremes between which virtue steers.

There was a long and ancient tradition of allegorical exposition of Homeric epics which is both older than and influenced Christian allegorical exegesis of Scripture of the sort we looked at in Chapter 2 (pp. 28–33). And Virgil's epic *Aeneid* was also read in this way. Such allegorization continued well into the Renaissance. A seventeenth-century translator of Ovid's Metamorphoses comments on Book XIV: 'The dangerous sailing between *Scylla* and *Charybdis*, commends the safetie of the middle course, and determres from either extremitie.'[2] The expression 'between Scylla and

Charybdis' was a common proverb, even cliché, in the sixteenth century and later. We can be sure Spenser read Homer's epics in this way,

> ...Homere, who in the Persons of Agamemnon and Vlysses hath ensampled a good gouernour and a vertuous man, the one in his Ilias, the other in his Odysseis...[3]

As we have seen, Spenser gave primacy to allegorical interpretation of Scripture in Book I. In Book II he turns to stories and motifs from a classical text which had long been allegorically interpreted, Homer's *Odyssey*. When Spenser read Scripture he also read within a tradition of allegorical exegesis of Scripture, so when he read classical narratives and myths he read them within an accumulated tradition of allegorical interpretation. His imitation of moments from the *Odyssey* participates in (and contributes to) a long tradition of allegorical readings of these stories. For example, Spenser's rewriting of Odysseus and Circe in Guyon and Acrasia strongly influences Milton, especially in his use of the same Homeric story in *Comus*. Milton was powerfully affected by *Faerie Queene*, II xii:

> Spenser...describing true temperance under the person of Guyon, brings him...through...the bower of earthly bliss, that he might see and know, and yet abstain.[4]

Milton's comment not only registers his reading of the journey through II xii, but also offers us an interpretation of it. For Milton the significance of Spenser's bringing Guyon through Acrasia's Bower is to show him and us something about true temperance, and about experience, knowledge and abstinence. I am now going to ask *you* for an interpretation of II xii.

This sounds (and is) a demanding project. In Chapter 1 of this *Guide* I quoted descriptions of allegorical reading as an 'endlesse' and incomplete work. Indeed, interpretation is an endless activity, but for the moment I want you to look particularly at one sort of possible reading of II xii. Chapter 5 of this *Guide* was often concerned with Dante's second traditional signification of allegory, the 'moral sense', from the chapter's epigraph from Lowell, to Aristotle's statement in his work on moral philosophy, the *Ethics*, that 'moral virtue is a mean'. We have seen that Book II is concerned with the moral and emotional life and with the virtue of temperance. **Following Guyon's journey in II xii, could you extract the 'moral' sense of the allegory, and, as a further exercise in temperate and disciplined restraint, write it down in about 200 words?**

I managed the following précis. The virtuous and temperate man steers a middle course between greed and waste (1–9). He avoids distraction, especially by empty and immodest trivia, and by extravagance (10–21). He is undaunted by fear (23–26) and also unmoved by pity (27–29). He ignores flattery and pleasant rest and is unmoved by neurotic anxieties. He rejects soft pleasure (46–49), is wary of beauty and delight (50–53), and rejects invitations of excess (54–57). He is steadfast in the face of the beautiful and the erotic (58–64), he (just) controls his sexual desire (64–69), and disciplines the reactions of sight and hearing to the attractions of beauty, even at its most delicate, artistic and poignant (70–78). The virtuous man must sometimes censor, imprison and destroy the pleasurable and beautiful.

Did you find this exercise easier for some parts of II xii than for others? Was it possible for *all* parts? Were you equally satisfied with the way you felt parts of such a summary conveyed your sense of the significance of different moments in II xii?

I found this a revealing exercise. Some moments seemed easier to sum up than others. The gulf and rock (1–9) were fairly straightforward because, although I suspect it is more complex than my reduction suggests, their signification is named for us as was Error's: 'Gulfe of Greedinesse' and 'Rock of Vile Reproach'. And the Palmer, as is his wont, spells out a signification of the gulf and rock (9). I notice that his 'luxurie' (indulgence) is a more general interpretation than my 'greed'. The quicksand 'Unthriftyhead' (extravagance) is similarly and revealingly named. The significance of the whirlpool 'Decay' is more difficult and diffuse. I am not sure either about the Hitchcockian birds and darkness. Is 'neurotic anxieties' overinterpretation of 34–37? I find that precision in moral interpretation gets more difficult as we near Acrasia's island and certainly as we approach the Bower. What do the mermaids offer and mean (30–34)? We land unobtrusively in 38, and after 42 precise moral commentary becomes really difficult. What can be said about 42–46? I cannot help feeling that my gloss of 46–49 is crude. I suppose that 'rejects invitations of excess' is fair as the moral sense of 54–57 but seems rough in dealing with this figure (as is Guyon?). The greatest problems I found were with the topography of the garden itself. What sort of moral gloss can be given for 42–45, 50–53 and 58–62? Looking back at my own moralizing précis above I see that after 58 it begins implicitly to appreciate Acrasia's garden, remarking on its beauty, delicacy and pathos. I had the greatest problem in my last sentence, where I thought that the verbs 'censor', 'imprison' and 'destroy' were accurate, but I realized it was difficult to find an object for them, that is, I was unsure what it *is* that Guyon censors, imprisons and destroys. To say 'the Bower', of course, simply shirks the difficulty. As you can see, I

settled for 'the pleasurable and beautiful'. Apparently a moral
interpretation of this canto has to cope with pleasures of reading
that the virtuous and temperate reader should reject or repress.
But even Guyon, who 'suffred no delight/To sincke into his sence,
nor mind affect' (xii 53.2–3), can also have his 'senses softly
tickeled' (xii 33.7) and can 'slacke his pace' at the sight of the
nymphs.

This brings us to a celebrated and continuing critical debate
about this canto. It is complex but, I think, may be fairly said to
hinge on what we are to do with pleasure, and especially the
pleasure of reading, in II xii. But I am assuming that readers
are offered pleasures in II xii. What are they? Some are more
obvious than others. The erotic display of the girls in the fountain
strikes most male readers forcibly. Acrasia herself offers more
sophisticated beauties and erotic artfulness. The aesthetic appeal
of the garden and Bower is strong. Acrasia's island offers imagined
sensuous satisfactions. It offers rest, art, sensuality, beauty, and
also more subtle pleasures of reading: the sense of an ending,
arrival, and finally the sense of a revelation of its central privacy
(77–79). **Please look closely at these stanzas. What pleasures do
they offer readers? Are these pleasures typical of those offered on
Acrasia's island?**

DISCUSSION

We are finally given the long-delayed sight of Acrasia, promised
since II i, our only previous glimpse coming in v 28–38. The
general mood is of heat, langour, relaxation, and of physical
invitation in the disposition of Acrasia's body (especially in
78.1–2). Rest and relaxation are two offers of Acrasia's garden.
Don't you find that the erotic invitation is more subtle than that of
the maidens in the fountain, although Acrasia's diaphanous silver
and silk also play their game of revealing and hiding? Acrasia's
beauty is a subtle mixture of nature and art, like that of her
garden (50, 58–59), the Porch of Excess (53–57) and the maidens
playing in the ornate fountain (60ff). It is confusing in that
although we can distinguish between nature and art in her skin
and silk veil, the skin itself is 'alablaster skin' which again blurs a
clear visual distinction between the physical and the artificial, just
as did the ivory waves on the gate to the garden (44–45). This
delicate veil calls forth as comparison an ominous allusion to the
deceit of craftsmanship in the spider's web, and to Arachne who
was transformed into a spider. But the stanza ends by decorating
this idea in a delicate picture of evanescent beauty in the morning

dewdrops on a spider's web. Beauty and pleasure made more precious by the quick passing of time were the subject of the song we have just heard in the garden (74–75).

The next stanza elaborates this picture, artfully reinforcing an implied sense of purity in 77 (alablaster, white, fine, deaw [dew]) again in 78 (snowy, drops, pure Orient perles). The picture of transient beauty is even more enthralling in 78.8–9. In stanza 79 Verdant provides a picture of adolescent male attractiveness and the same sense of sweetness and freshness, but also of defaced nobility. I think that stanzas 77–79 sum up in a refined and alluring form the pleasures of Acrasia's garden: eroticism, beauty and especially the aesthetic appeal of beauty and art of a high order, rest and sensuality.

But stanza 79 also warns about the effects of Acrasia in whatever is happening to Verdant. And, of course, going along with the Bower's evocations of extraordinary beauty and pleasure, there is the basis for the moral commentary we produced earlier in adjectives such as 'frail', 'lavish', 'fowle', 'wanton', 'lascivious' and 'horrible'. Do you think that they are enough to control and warn convincingly against the Bower's attractions?

Because of its extraordinary power, beauty and pleasure for the reader this canto obviously poses a number of difficult questions. Can you accept that Guyon is right to chain up Acrasia and destroy her Bower? If readers agree that the Bower must be destroyed, must the knight of temperance do it so aggressively and wholeheartedly? 'Rigour pittilesse' and 'the tempest of his wrathfulnesse' are Spenser's description (83). What, some critics have asked, is Spenser's position? Does he approve of the knight of temperance's behaviour and actions? Or is he secretly (or not so secretly) attached to the beauty, sensuous appeal, delicacy and artfulness of Acrasia's Bower, the product of her art, but also *his* as a poet? Is Spenser like Archimago after he has fashioned the False Una, 'The maker selfe for all his wondrous witt,/Was nigh beguiled with so goodly sight'?

I think that you might usefully consider such questions in the context of some of the history of more general critical appreciation of Spenser, not just of the Bower. We have seen something of Milton's response to what he saw as Spenser's moral didacticism: his declaration that Spenser is a better teacher than medieval theologians, his liking for Book II and its instruction in temperance and abstinence. Eighteenth-century readers thought of Spenser as a poet of the 'fancy' or of the imagination. Romantic critics and nineteenth-century readers often spoke of Spenser as a dreamer and of his poetry as dreams, and this is the way he often appears in some romantic poems. In the nineteenth century, partly because of a taste for the sensuous appeal of romantic poetry, 'pleasure' is thought to be the most typical characteristic of Spenser's poetry. Here are some fragments from nineteenth-century critics on Spenser' poetry:

> ... it is inspired by the love of ease, and relaxation from all the cares and business of life ... voluptuousness of sentiment ... The love of beauty, however, and not of truth, is the moving principle of his mind ...

> He is, of all our poets, the most truly sensuous ... The delicious abundance and overrunning luxury of Spenser appear in the very structure of his verse.

> ... labyrinth of beauty, a forest of old romance in which it is possible to lose oneself more irrecoverably amid the tangled luxury of loveliness than elsewhere in English poetry.

> He is a poet of the delighted senses, and his song becomes most beautiful when he writes of those islands of Phaedria and Acrasia ...[5]

Ease, relaxation, voluptuousness, sensuous, beauty, luxury. Don't you think that readers in the nineteenth century seem to be describing Spenser's poetry in terms unnervingly like those which might describe our experience of the Bower of Bliss? The last extract, from W. B. Yeats, who edited a selection of extracts from Spenser and whose poetry was strongly influenced by him, makes explicit an analogy between the pleasure of Spenser's poetry and of Acrasia's garden. And in Yeats Spenser appears not only as the poet of the delighted senses but also as the poet of pleasure in conflict with an official and impersonal morality he is obliged to express, and which resulted in 'that conflict between the aesthetic and moral interests that was to run through well nigh all his works'.[6]

The particular critical problems of the Bower, and more general critical doubts about *Faerie Queene*, Book II, were put concisely by Grierson in 1929. **Do you agree with him? How far are you prepared to go along with his argument? What do you think are its strong or weak features?**

> And what of the moral allegory of the second book? The babe with the bloody hands, the House of Medina and her sisters, Pyrochles and Furor and Occasion; does any one of these leave an impression on the imagination to counterbalance the sensuous beauty of the Bower of Immodest Mirth, or the Bower of Bliss, or the Song of the Rose, which Spenser translated from Tasso ... [quotes II xii 74–75]. I know that Milton and Professor de Selincourt [editor of Spenser's *Works*] assure us that in the description of the Bower of Bliss the poet displays the charm of the sensuous in order to emphasise the stern morality which destroys the Bower. But this is not quite

relevant. The senses have their legitimate claims. There is no virtue
in the mere destruction of the beautiful. The moralist must convince
us that the sacrifice is required in the interest of what is a higher and
more enduring good, that the sensuous yields place to the spiritual.
It is this Spenser fails to do imaginatively, whatever doctrine one
may extract intellectually from the allegory.[7]

DISCUSSION

I think that we have to agree with Grierson that there is nothing
in Book II to compare with the imaginative power of canto xii. I
suppose the cave of Mammon is a sombre rival for leaving an
impression on the imagination. Grierson does not mention this,
but then I do not think it allures us with 'sensuous beauty' in any
way like the Bower. In fact it is forbidding where the Bower is
inviting. The Bower and the Cave of Mammon are alike in their
sequence of thresholds passed through, their gardens, and their
offers of things to be consumed which are resisted by Guyon.
But they are sensationally unlike in that Mammon's Cave offers
temptations which are more easily rejected because they are
aesthetically less appetizing: they are sombre, gloomy and metallic.
Do you think perhaps that the portrait of Belpheobe (iii 22ff)
could be said imaginatively to 'counterbalance . . . sensual beauty'?
This picture, too, is certainly beautiful, delicately erotic, and
aesthetically appealing in its elaborate artifice. You might usefully
try a close comparison of Acrasia and Belphoebe in order to test
Grierson's assertion. Belphoebe's graceful courage and her praise
of the active life are the opposite of the restful langour with which
the garden mixes its beauty (and so increases its attraction?). I am
not sure whether Guyon's and the reader's moral alertness are
'lulled' by the beauty and pleasure of the poetry. If I am aware
that I am being lulled, at least, like Guyon, do I not have a sort of
internal Palmer to tell me that this is so? I think that my more
uneasy suspicion is not that I unknowingly might be full of sleep
when I lose the right way, but that I might turn out to be Verdant
– or even Grill – and consent knowingly to the garden's attractions
and hence to my own transformation. Alternatively, perhaps if I
am as hoggishly minded as the Palmer thinks Grill is (87) then, of
course, I would not have the discrimination to know whether I
was being lulled or not.

I think that Grierson is most compelling towards the end of
this paragraph: 'The senses have their legitimate claims. There is
no virtue in the mere destruction of the beautiful'. It is around
Guyon's rejection of pleasure and his destruction of beauty that

the debate revolves. One answer that still permeates criticism of II xii is that of C. S. Lewis. We may feel that what happens in the Bower is that readers are shown pleasure and beauty and then have them denied, repressed and destroyed. Lewis argued that attentive readers could see that they were not real pleasure and beauty anyway. He argued that the Bower offered art and nature in conflict, vulgarity not beauty, voyeurism not sexual satisfaction, 'artifice, sterility and death'. Since Lewis's argument has been influential you should read it to see how much you can agree with and use it as a way of defining your own critical assessment of II xii.[8] The critical debate about Acrasia's garden in which we are participating still continues and the note at the end of this paragraph directs you to some contributions to it.[9]

I want to leave the particularities of Acrasia's garden and widen the discussion to some issues in Renaissance poetry in general and allegory in particular. They are issues to do with the belief, from the Renaissance and much earlier, that poetry can and ought to teach, that it can be the agent of moral and philosophical ideas, which are raised and conveyed in the legend of temperance.

I want you now to look at some of 'A Preface, or Rather a Briefe Apologie of Poetrie' which is prefaced to Sir John Harington's translation of the Italian poet Ariosto's romance *Orlando Furioso* (1591). Ariosto's chivalric romance poem was published in its final form in 1532 and is mentioned by Spenser in the Letter to Ralegh (Penguin edition, p. 15). We will come back to it in the next chapter. Harington's translation came out a year after the publication of the first three books of the *Faerie Queene* and, like Spenser's poem, it was dedicated to Queen Elizabeth. In his 'Preface' Harington offers allegorical theory couched in highly metaphorical terms. Then, 'for making the matter plaine' he gives as an illustrative example a sequence of allegorical readings of the myth of the Greek hero, Perseus, who killed the Gorgon, a monster with snakes for hair whose glance turned men to stone. You can read a telling of this myth in Ovid, *Metamorphoses*, Book IV,[10] and would find it interesting, as parts of it are an analogue to the story of George and the dragon which is, of course, the framework of *Faerie Queene*, Book I. I have pruned Harington's allegorical interpretations in the spirit of a reason he gives himself: 'The like infinite Allegories I could pike out . . . save that I would avoid tediousnes'. Look at his treatment of classical myth in the light of our examination of treatment of the story of Odysseus in this chapter. And what do you make of his metaphors for the relation of poetry and meaning, and for allegory?

The ancient Poets have indeed wrapped as it were in their writings divers [several] and sundry meanings, which they call the senses or mysteries theereof. First of all for the litterall sence (as it were the utmost barke or ryne [rind]) they set downe in manner of an historie the acts and notable exploits of some persons worthy memorie: then in the same fiction, as a second rine and somewhat more fine, as it were nearer to the pith and marrow, they place the Morall sence profitable for the active life of man, approving vertuous actions and condemning the contrarie. Manie times also under the selfesame words they comprehend some true understanding of naturall Philosophie [physics], or sometimes of politike governement, and now and then of divinitie: and these same sences that comprehend so excellent knowledge we call the Allegorie, which *Plutarch* defineth to be when one thing is told, and by that another is understood . . . for making the matter more plaine I will alledge an example thereof.

Perseus sonne of Jupiter is fained by the Poets to have slaine *Gorgon*, and, after that conquest atchieved, to have flown up to heaven. The Historicall sence is this, *Perseus* the sonne of *Jupiter*, by the participation of *Jupiters* vertues which were in him, . . . slew *Gorgon*, a tyrant . . . and was for his vertuous parts exalted by men up unto heaven. Morally it signifieth this much: *Perseus* a wise man, . . . endewed with vertue from above, slayeth sinne and vice, . . . and so mounteth up to the skie of vertue . . . It hath also another Theologicall Allegorie . . .[11]

Harington interprets the story of Perseus as generations of interpreters, including Spenser, interpreted Odysseus. In addition, you may have noticed that apparently classical myth was made to yield up successive layers of different sorts of interpretation in the same way that Dante extracted polysemous meanings from the verse from Psalms.

In Chapter 2 we saw that some metaphors for allegory were veils, mirrors, books (all objects of visual perception, which itself in Western thought tends to be the dominant metaphor for mental perception). Here the metaphor, like that of the veil, is partly one of coverings (Harington's 'wrapped' and '*under* the selfsame words'), then successive layers of wrapping which cover and lie ever nearer the centre ('utmost barke or ryne' . . . 'a second rine and somewhat more fine, as it were nearer to the pith and marrow'). Here you probably also noticed Harington's 'Morall sence' instructive of virtue and the active life. But I think that the metaphor also implies the idea of a fruit to be eaten: we have already seen reading as ingestion and consumption in the case of Error (see p. 9). Like the metaphors of mirror and veil, the metaphor of allegory as a fruit with many husks or skins is very common. The image also expresses the relation of surface and substance.

The relation of surface and substance, and possible dis-
crepancies between them, was a preoccupation of the Renaissance
in general. It is constantly voiced in Shakespeare's plays: 'Oh what
a goodly *outside* falsehood hath' says Antonio.[12] Spenser is aware
of the possibility of this discrepancy in the first stanza of the
Proem to Book II. Some readers will think his poem a 'painted
forgery'. We have seen something of the general fear that representations may deceive, and how truth appears or may be
falsified, in Chapter 3. There I suggested that the art of the
magician, Archimago, is analogous to the poet's: both may deceive
in their representations, and earlier in this chapter I again compared Spenser the poet to Archimago, and implicitly to Acrasia
(pp. 37–8, 83–4).

The prime problem of Renaissance criticism was the justification of fiction itself: an acute case of the anxiety about representation. There had always been those who said that fiction was
deception and worse still highly pleasurable deception which at
best distracted mankind from virtue, at worst actively enticed it
to vice. Those who defended fiction against such attacks, and
Sir Philip Sidney is its most famous sixteenth-century English
defender, said that, on the contrary, fiction instructed us to virtue
and its function was 'to teach and delight'.[13] Fiction's justification
was that it taught virtue with greater persuasive power than any
discipline such as history or moral philosophy, and it did this
because it 'delighted' through the pleasure it gave. What makes
fiction uniquely powerful, and provides its justification for the
Renaissance, is the pleasure of the text. But paradoxically it was
various kinds of pleasure that had long laid fiction open to attack
by those who distrusted pleasure and fiction. Sidney reports these
objections against poetry: 'it is the nurse of abuse, infecting us
with many pestilent desires, with a siren's sweetness drawing the
mind . . . it abuseth men's wit, training it to wanton sinfulness and
lustful love'. He also argues for fiction's unique power delightfully
to persuade men to virtue: 'and delight to move men to take that
goodness in hand, which without delight they would fly as from a
stranger'.[14] If, like Guyon, a reader 'yet suffred no delight/To
sincke into his sence, nor mind affect' (xii 53.2–3), fiction could
not proceed with its task delightfully to instruct.

I have given this brief and rather crude exposition of an
aspect of Renaissance discussion of poetry so that you might
reconsider Acrasia's garden and fundamental questions of the
relations of instruction, pleasure and reading from another point
of view. I would now like you to consider our experience as
readers of Acrasia's garden in relation to two passages. The first is

a simile from Sidney's *Apology for poetry* (printed in 1595) in which he compares the delightful instruction of fiction to a doctor administering sweetened medicine:

> even as the child is often brought to take most wholesome things by hiding them in such other as have a pleasant taste...[15]

The second is from Castiglione's manual for Italian courtiers, *The Book of the Courtier* (first printed in 1528), in which one of the courtiers describes how a courtier might delightfully instruct his prince in virtue.

> In this wise may hee leade him through the rough way of vertue (as it were) decking it aboute with boughes to shadow it, and strowing it over with sightlye [beautiful] flowers, to ease the griefe of the painefull jorney in him that is but of a weake force. And sometime with musicke, sometime with armes, and horses, sometime with rymes and meeter, otherwhile with communication of love, ... continually keepe that minde of his occupied in honest pleasure: imprinting notwithstanding therein alwaies beside (as I have saide) in company with these flickering provocations some vertuous condition, and beguiling him with a holesom craft as the warie [careful] Phisitions doe, who many times when they minister to yong and tender children in their sicknesse, a medicine of a bitter taste, annoint the cup about the brimme with some sweete licour.[16]

I would like you at the end of this chapter to think of these metaphors concerned with the relation of surface and substance and pleasure and instruction in fiction: Harington's layers wrapped around the pith and the fruit and its rind, Castiglione's rough way of virtue shadowed with trees and flowers, and Sidney and Castiglione's medicine hidden under a pleasant taste or in a cup with a sweetened rim. And I would like you then to consider them in relation to Acrasia's garden. **Can you find these images and ideas manifested in the Bower of Bliss? What conclusions do you think are possible about 'fiction' in Acrasia's garden?**

I am aware of guiding your thoughts quite strongly in a certain direction here, but I think you might find these ideas useful as an approach to this episode crucial for both the *Faerie Queene* and debate about Spenser's poetry in general. These metaphors about fiction, allegory and 'holesom craft', as Hoby's translation of Castiglione calls it, permeate the description and language of Acrasia's garden. The whole garden itself is, of course, decked with boughs, shade and flowers and through it Guyon makes his effortful journey on the 'rough way of vertue'. This discourse of the healthful instruction of fiction (sweet pleasure on the surface, fruit and rind, etc.) is in terms perilously close to those of Acrasia's

garden. Even if we think that the pleasures of Acrasia's garden are
dishonest or enfeebling, aren't the terms for honest and dishonest
use of pleasure interchangeable?

The metaphor of the delightful sweetness of fiction is applicable to the surface delights of Acrasia's garden. It is worth
investigating the occurrences of both 'sweetness' and 'delight' in
II xii. But is it the case that in Acrasia's garden a surface of
sweetened fiction hides not the medicine of instruction, but the
poison of vice? And the metaphors of allegory are appropriate to
Acrasia's garden: text and sub-text, surface and meaning, delight
and meaning. The metaphors of husk and nut, rind and fruit,
sugar coating the medicine remind me of the constant invitation to
taste that the garden offers. **How are these invitations to taste
used? Why are they rejected by Guyon? On what grounds?**

Harington's sense of allegory as a sense of increasing pen-
etration to truth is also suggestive. The initiatory stages of Guyon
in his underground journey to and through the House of Mammon
are repeated in the knight's crossing of thresholds, passing through
doors in Acrasia's garden. Already in the eighteenth century
Guyon's journey through the cave of Mammon was thought of as
an initiation. The sense of penetrating towards the inner mystery
of truth is parodied (or simply replicated?) in the gradual pen-
etration of Acrasia's garden until we see the final revelation of the
witch herself.

It might be possible to see Acrasia's garden as a parody not
only of (or just a comparison with?) paradise, but of Renaissance
ideas and justifications of the operation of poetry itself. In Acrasia
we might choose to see a demonic parody of the allegorist. Alternatively, does the poet fashioning this poem use the same artistic
practices as his demonic parody so that, as Milton put it, 'we
might see, know and yet abstain'? Acrasia's beauty is the sort that
artists create. Her final appearance is like a self-staged painterly
tableau. Arguably the poet replicates Acrasia's own abuse of art so
that we might temperately reject such an abuse.

Sidney justifies pleasure by stressing the teaching. Cannot the
pleasurable fictions of the poets be ends in themselves? Is there,
then, a sort of schizophrenic division of the function of poetry
in the Bower, where the surface delight and sweetness actually
persuade to the very opposite of virtuous instruction? This would
be a way of restating the nineteenth- and indeed twentieth-century
ideas about the division between the moralist and the poet: 'the
poet's innate voluptuousness is in constant antagonism with his
earnest protestant, almost puritanical creed'.[17]

At the very least, I think that we could say that this text must at least be aware of the possibility of the abuse of the surface sweetness of fiction. The end of Book II is acutely conscious of both the use and abuse of allegory. And it is the poem's increasingly self-conscious scrutiny of literature and of itself which we will find continues in Book III.

7. Romance

'. . . the great valiance of noble Gentlemen, the terrible combates of couragious personages, the vertuous mindes of noble Dames, the chaste hartes of constant Ladyes, the wonderful patience of puissant Princes, the mild sufferaunce of well disposed gentlewomen, . . .'

(William Painter, *The Palace of Pleasure* 1566[1])

Read *Faerie Queene*, Book III, making the usual general notes. At a first reading you may find it more than usually hard to keep track of the narratives and characters of this book. Is it more difficult in this book to follow the stories and keep track of the characters than in the two previous books? If so, why? How does it compare with these earlier books in its quest and the attention paid to its patron knight?

DISCUSSION

It is undoubtedly more difficult, I think. We begin by supposing that the book of chastity will be mainly concerned with the career of the virtue's patron knight, Britomart, as the previous books were largely concerned with the quest of Redcrosse (even when *he* forgot it) and of the determined Guyon. Instead, she is absent from the central section of the book. Even allowing for the poem's love of digression, which we considered in Chapter 4, our direct access to the knight of chastity seems more than usually intermittent. We encounter her in the present in III i, but already from ii 17 to iii 62 we are hearing of her in retrospect, with the added temporal complication that in iii 22–49 we hear Merlin's prophecy of the future and of Britomart's descendants. After overthrowing Marinell she is absent from Book III from iv 18 until she enters again unexpectedly as an unknown (male) knight in ix 12, who is revealed to be female and Britomart at ix 20ff. She only takes up the narrative initiative again at xi 6.

And both when Britomart is present and when she is not we are given many other narratives whose intrinsic interest is hard to keep in mind, as our attention is demanded by one character then another and by proliferating digressions in which new characters and also many figures from the previous two books appear (Redcrosse, Satyrane, Braggadocchio, Belphoebe). If the quest is a means of structuring a book and providing it with its purpose and expected end, what *is* the quest of the knight of chastity and does she achieve it? It is certainly not her experience in the House of Busirane which, although it comes at the end of the book (like Redcrosse's fight with the Dragon and Guyon's temptations in Acrasia's garden), is an unexpected adventure Britomart undertakes only in III xi. And what relation do all the many other stories apparently competing for the reader's attention have to the virtue of chastity, the 'fairest vertue, farre aboue the rest' (Proem 1.2)?

In Chapter 4 I suggested the musical technique of 'counterpoint' as a way of thinking about the integral relevance of apparent digressions in Book I. I find that a related musical term, 'polyphony', which is an extension of this technique, is useful in thinking about Book III. Polyphony [literally 'many voices'] is *several* voices counterpointing each other, two, three or more sounding at the same time, and is a formal characteristic of much Renaissance music. One Elizabethan choral work by the composer Thomas Tallis takes polyphony to extraordinary lengths and asks for forty voices.[2] To hear how polyphony sounds you could try listening to recordings of certain sorts of English Renaissance music for voices: the masses of the Elizabethan composer William Byrd or some Elizabethan madrigals would give you an impression.[3] In polyphony we are aware of and can follow the individual musical lines for voices (soprano, alto, tenor and bass) independently pursuing their own vocal lines across the page as they sing 'horizontally' to the piece's end. But also at any one moment in the music we hear 'vertically' the harmony of the one blended sound of the voices sounding together. So at any one moment in the progress of Book III, as well as being (roughly) aware of the location, progress and state of, say, Britomart, Florimell and Belphoebe, we have a general sense of the 'voices' of their present situations in the poem contributing to a more complex sound composed of separate but superimposed voices. So the significance of the allegorical 'harmony' at one moment in the poem is composed, say, of Britomart searching for Arthegall, Florimell imprisoned by Proteus, and Belphoebe caring for the wounded Timias.

As a way of beginning to tease apart the polyphonic narratives of Book III, I want in the course of this chapter to ask you to spend some time following and examining the career of Florimell, which provides one of the 'voices' of Book III from her appearance in Canto i to her imprisonment in Canto viii. We will start with her sudden appearance in the poem, and also with an example of intertextuality. I would like you to read some extracts from the first canto of Sir John Harington's translation of a long sixteenth-century Italian chivalric romance, Ariosto's *Orlando Furioso*. You have already encountered some of Harington's preface to his translation in Chapter 6. At the beginning of Ariosto's poem the knight, Rinaldo, and his cousin, Orlando, are rivals for the love of the beautiful Angelica. Angelica flees from an attack on Charlemagne's camp and from her suitors. Here is part of the description of her headlong flight:

> But she that shuns *Renaldo* all she may,
>   Upon her horses necke doth lay the raine,
>   Through thicke and thin she gallopeth away
>   Ne makes the choice of beaten way or plaine,
>   But gives her palfrey leave to chuse the way,
>   And being mov'd with feare and with disdaine,
>   Now up, now downe, she never leaves to ride,
>   Till she arrived by a river side.
>   . . .
>
> [She] fled through woods and deserts all obscure,
>   Through places uninhabited and wast,
>   Ne could she yet repute her selfe secure,
>   But farther still she gallopeth in hast.
>   Eache leafe that stirres in her doth feare procure,
>   And maketh her affrighted and agast:
>   Each noise she heares, each shadow she doth see,
>   She doth mistrust it should Renaldo be.
>
> Like to a fawne, or kid of bearded goate,
>   That in the wood a tyger fierce espide,
>   To kill her dam, and first to teare the throate,
>   And then to feed upon the hanch or side,
>   Both feare lest she might light on such a lot,

And seeke it selfe in thickest brackes to hide,
And thinkes each noise the wind or aire doth cause,
It selfe in danger of the tygers clawes.

That day and night she wandred here and there,
And halfe the other day that did ensue,
Untill at last she was arrived where
A fine young grove . . .[4]

Now, in about 50 or 60 words make a brief précis of your impression of Angelica and of the simile used of her. And what do you make of the appropriateness of this simile? I would like you to use this brief summary as a point of reference in our discussion of Florimell.

DISCUSSION

Here is my summary: Angelica is in constant and directionless flight from one man, Rinaldo. Her flight is caused by fear and haughtiness ('feare and with disdaine'). She is in constant fear, terrified by every noise, which she thinks is the approaching Rinaldo. The simile compares her to a mother animal or its female young, prey to a tiger. I asked you to consider the appropriateness of the simile because it was at this point that it struck me that I was not at all sure what Harington's translation of Ariosto was doing with it. The images of frightened and vulnerable female animals are appropriate. A fawn aptly conjures up a defenceless and delicate young animal, but I am not sure about the 'kid of bearded goate'.[5] The threatened violence is graphic, with its imagination of a torn throat and side, but isn't it overdone? Is this really how Angelica sees her pursuing knightly suitor? I said that you should keep this passage in mind as a point of reference for a discussion of Florimell. I am also asking you to bear in mind the point of view from which we see Angelica, and how Angelica views her pursuers.

Now read carefully and closely III i 14–20. Look first at how the 'goodly Ladie' is presented to the reader in the way with which you are now familiar in this *Guide*. What do you think her brief appearance signifies? You should bear in mind your previous exercises in reading other Spenserian female figures (such as Una, Duessa, Acrasia). Then look also at the presentation of the forester.

DISCUSSION

The irruption of this lady into the poem is sudden and unexpected and shatters the harmonious, untroubled and slow progress of stanza 14, although there are hints about the savagery of the forest in 14.5–7. The picture in stanza 15 seems to flash by almost too quickly for us to notice (15.9), but our privilege as readers is, of course, to be able to freeze the frame and replay it as often as we wish. Our impressions of the lady are imaginatively asserted to be the same as those of the group of knightly spectators.

Even though we are all now seasoned readers of the poem's female figures, I think that this one's significance is particularly elusive. She is another Spenserian 'goodly Ladie', a formula which by now we trust to tell us absolutely nothing except to exercise more than usual care in our reading about truth and representation. (You will remember that 'goodly Lady' is used of Duessa, I ii 13.2). Her milk-white mount is perhaps reassuring in that it is like Una's ass, but like Duessa this lady rides a palfrey. Her solitariness and fear make her the object of our compassion. Her terrified speed is unlike Una's sober deliberation, but neither is it like Duessa's jaunty pace. The impression is one of beauty, of purity in whiteness, but also fragility. Her beauty is that of precious but fragile substances: crystal, whalebone, thinly beaten gold, tinsel. She is all white and gold like a fairy-tale princess. The only part of her body we see is her face and that, because of fear, is in the simile 'as white as whales bone' (15.5). The general personal impression of this lady in i 15 is of speed, purity, preciousness, fragility and fear. The next stanza elaborates the fear and speed. The backward gaze fixed on some evil is the more chilling because the evil is unspecified in this stanza. 'As fearing evil' produces the usual ambiguity: this woman fears evil or is figuratively *like one* who fears evil. Her hair is like a comet, an appropriate comparison for the lady's swiftness, brightness, and also for the poem's original readers a sign of disturbance and change, as 16.7–9 makes clear.

The forester is grotesque, grisly and beastly, driven by a crude obsession which monomaniacally drives him to spur his horse on to exhaustion.[6] His limited and crude vision expresses itself in the series of tired, clichéd doublets ('thicke and thin', etc.) in 17.5–6. This characterless forester, never to be named, is a figure in whom individuation has collapsed into an overriding obsession. He sees only the sexual object of the woman in front of him. He consists only of self-driven and panting exhaustion, huge limbs, clumsy hands and a phallic boar-spear.

When working on your analysis of the poem's presentation of these two figures, I expect that you were also aware that when you were establishing your own view of these figures there is a multiplicity of viewpoints available on these events internally in the poem. In these stanzas more than one pair of eyes is watching the lady's flight and pursuit, from the time she gallops into the canto in stanza 15 to when she leaves it as rapidly in stanza 20. I would like you now to look more closely at this variety of viewpoints and their relation to your own. Can you say something about the viewpoints in these stanzas? Think about the ways all these different eyes see the lady and the forester. Are these ways all the same? And how does she see the figures who are gazing at her? You might find it useful to think of this small scene as one from a film. Where is the Spenserian 'camera' at different points in these stanzas? Who is looking at whom? Start this time with the forester.

DISCUSSION

The poem is at pains to remind us that the reader's gaze is shared by other spectators (15.9, 17.1). In stanzas 15–16 the viewpoint seems a general one we share with the spectators in the poem. But after a momentary breather in 17.1, we shift focus from the lady to the cause of her fear in her would-be rapist, the forester. I have suggested a brief reading of him, but whose viewpoint am I describing here? Obviously my own, but I think that this view of mine in part incorporates a sense of the forester which the text mediates to me as Florimell's. Her constant backward stare (16.1) makes me think that it is particularly *her* sight of her pursuer which I am given in stanza 17. It is her frightened ear that records the panting, her terrified gaze zooms in on (and so in her fear exaggerates?) those huge limbs and clumsy hands and picks out in close-up the sexually aggressive detail of the boar-spear.

If Florimell's terrified gaze is partly responsible for the text's construction of the forester (that is, her fear and flight construct his crude breathless desire and threateningly rough male body), perhaps the nature of his aggressive desire has to do with a woman's appearance in this canto as pure, brittle, agitated and in terrified flight. Male lust and female fearful flight symbiotically construct each other.

And what is the viewpoint at the beginning of stanza 18? Apparently that of the spectating knights: 'Which outrage when those gentle knights did see' (18.1). Florimell sees the forester, her spectators see outrage. This moment of static inspection is immediately gone in the headlong dispersal of knights in stanza 18. In this stanza we undoubtedly zoom back to view from the middle distance the effect of looking at the lady's flight on at least three of her male spectators. Arthur and Guyon gallop off in pursuit of the lady and Timias in pursuit of the forester. But what motivates this second male pursuit of a woman? 'Outrage' at the sight of an attempted rape is to be expected as something we can share with them, but we are told that the pursuit of Florimell by Arthur and Guyon is prompted by 'great enuie and fell gealosy' (18.2). Now although we can gloss these abstract nouns with sixteenth-century meanings of respectively 'hostility' and 'indignation', even in the sixteenth century the words also had their current senses of envy and jealousy, implying in the knights a community of erotic desire with the forester. The watching knights could want to pursue Florimell for reasons like (but we hope not identical with) those of the forester. In spite of the obvious differences between the forester (peasant, grotesque, crude) and the knights (aristocratic, personable, refined), they have desires in common. Florimell (rightly?) cannot distinguish between them and will spend a great deal of time in Book III in flight from all male pursuit.

On the evidence of these stanzas we might have not only a polyphony of narratives in Book III, but also a polyphony of viewpoints which constitute our sense of this particular episode. **Are we made to feel that any one is more desirable than the others?**

DISCUSSION

The flight of Florimell actually has five male spectators: the forester, Arthur, Guyon, Timias and the Palmer whose reactions we are not given and whom we have forgotten about. Presumably his reason is unaffected by the spectacle. And there is one female spectator, Britomart. But by now we are used to the poem offering us and encouraging us to a certain *specularity* on its episodes and figures, that is, a superior and panoramic viewpoint for the reader which is not usually that of any one figure or group of figures in the poem, and which we experience as that which the text encourages us to have. At least, it is usually superior to that of any character or group of characters. Perhaps there are exceptions. Are Arthur and Una two of these? So, for example, whose opinion do you think the poem thinks is worth having about

Acrasia's Bower of Bliss: Gryll's, Verdant's, Cymochles's, Acrasia's, Guyon's . . . ? Given the discussion at the end of Chapter 6, I think the answer would have to be a careful one, but I am almost sure that it is not Gryll's or Acrasia's. But neither would I be entirely happy with Guyon's. Of course, I am most (dangerously?) pleased with whatever view I have formed as a reader in response to the text.

In stanza 18 we zoom out from close shots of the lady and the hotly pursuing forester to pan across five figures now in rapid and dispersed movement, and achieve a detached readerly specularity. But this is only to find in stanza 19 that this final panoramic specularity and readerly superiority is also and already ('The whiles . . .') that of Britomart. Her calm speculation apparently allows her the sort of detached reflection the reader is also capable of. And more than that, the first two lines of this stanza reveal that this specularity provides her and us with an allegorical reading of the episode we have just witnessed:

> The whiles faire *Britomart*, whose constant mind,
> Would not so lightly follow beauties chace

In 'beauties chace' this short allegorical pageant offers us a concise reduction of its signification in a phrase which itself is an illustration of Aristotle's point about 'ordinary' language often being metaphorical. To put it another way, the scene in i 15–19 is an allegorical elaboration (Puttenham's 'long and perpetuall Metaphore') of the words 'beauties chace'. One signification of the rapid pageant we have just witnessed is an allegorical representation of the pursuit of beauty. This beauty puts into motion its pursuit by varieties of male desire. Britomart's consciousness of the episode as 'beauties chace' articulates a further and superior reading of this episode as it was a Renaissance commonplace, deriving ultimately from Plato and expressed later in Book III, that love is a desire for beauty ('that sweet fit, that doth true beautie loue', iii 1.7). It seems, then, an extraordinary feature of Britomart that the poem attributes to her consciousness the kernel of the allegorical meaning of the episode we have just collectively witnessed. This, I think, makes her an extraordinary figure in the poem and suggests the expression in Book III of a detached and sophisticated specularity we have not encountered before, or encountered only as possible in *our* view as readers of the poem, not in its characters. I will return to this point in the next chapter.

Let us now pursue Florimell. Using your notes, first extract the broad outlines of Florimell's story from Book III. What are its

episodes? In these episodes what kind of experience does Florimell
have of male figures?

DISCUSSION

We have already examined our first flashing sight of Florimell at
i 15–19. After her disappearance in Canto i, Florimell's next
appearance, which comes after Marinell has been wounded by
Britomart, is appropriately and tantalizingly rapid in iv 45–53,
pursued by Arthur and Guyon. After that her story is continued in
III vii–viii. Florimell seems singularly unlucky in the men with
whom she comes into close contact and attracts a series of un-
desirable admirers: a panting country boor with large hands (III i);
the lazy, brutish son of a witch (III vii); an almost impotent but
nevertheless sexually predatory old fisherman; and finally an old,
cold, rough-bearded sea-god (III viii). In them Florimell's night-
mare (fantasy?) of male pursuit and violation, which we might
guess at from our first rapid sight of her, become more and more
real. Whatever the significance the (male) hyena has, it is yet
another example of the threat in Book III to pursue, violate and
now devour Florimell. In Cantos vii–viii she escapes from the
hyena only to be threatened by an old fisherman, the Spenserian
equivalent of an old man in a dirty raincoat. Her fears seem
gradually realized as every male creature she meets is a potential
sexual aggressor. Let us look closer at these encounters.

In III iv 45–53 we find Florimell still in flight, now from Arthur
and Guyon. How does the lady see the knights, and the knights
the lady, in these few stanzas, and how do we see all of them?
Look closely at the language and images in stanza 46. How do
they affect our consideration of this question? And what effect is
Florimell's flight and pursuit having on the number and variety of
narratives in Book III?

DISCUSSION

In this episode Florimell is pursued by Arthur, whom she escapes
as night comes on. The metaphor of the hunt of love continues the
idea of the pursuit of Florimell in i 15–19, and is used with witty
relentlessness. Florimell is a hare (46.4) and then a dove pursued
by a male falcon (49.4–9) The first line of stanza 46 echoes the
doublet clichés previously used of the forester. The simile of the
lady pursued by men as a hare hunted by hounds is aggressive in
its threat of violence. Is this simile expressing just Florimell's view
of the situation, or is its point of view one we should adopt as

accurate? Surely this stanza allows a double view of the pursuit of Florimell. In her terror she may see her male pursuers here (Arthur and Guyon) as hunters and hounds. On the other hand 'incessant paines' (46.3) pays tribute to their efforts on her behalf. Or are these pains just the unrelenting and constant urgings of their desires? From Florimell's harassed and fearful viewpoint Arthur and Guyon are 'houndes trew' (46.5) in that they are all too doggedly sure of the scent, but we may also think them 'trew' (trusty, reliable) as their pursuit is in defence and aid of her chastity, and they intend her 'reskew' (46.7) not her violation. In this they are unlike many knights in Ariosto, who as a reward for saving a lady's chastity (especially Angelica's) expect that *they* might be the privileged violator. We might then say that Florimell in her flight has nervously in mind the possible predicaments of Angelica, her Ariostan prototype. Florimell's effect on her male pursuers is to disperse them and consequently their narratives more and more widely over Book III. There is further parting of the ways as Arthur and Guyon go in different directions and Timias still pursues the forester (46–47). Now three male narrative lines go their 'three sundry wayes' (47.5). Florimell's flight generates an increasingly complex polyphony in the narratives of Book III, and will cause yet further confusion and dispersal of the knights in Books III and IV. As Florimell's flight from the forester called into being the dispersed quests of Authur, Guyon and Timias, so her flight from the hyena in III vii will call into the poem an old fisherman, Satyrane, the giantess Argante and her brother Ollyphant, the squire Argante had captured, and the knight pursuing the giantess.

In part we have just been considering here masculine and feminine points of view, or how we might interpret key phrases ('incessant paines', 'houndes trew') from the viewpoints of differently gendered figures in the poem. **Look now at the last set of Florimell's experiences in this book, in III viii, with the old fisherman and with Proteus. By the end of III viii, could it be that with so many men pursuing Florimell the poem is treating her comically? Do you agree? If so, what sorts of humour are being deployed? Do you feel at all uneasy about such humour? What bearing might this scene have on questions of masculine and feminine points of view?**

DISCUSSION

It seems to me that in Canto viii Florimell is the prey of (specifically masculine?) comedy and irony as the episode in the boat is full of sexual and particularly phallic innuendo which erupts into sexual aggression against her. There are sexual double-meanings – to 'play' (20.3), 'courage' and 'stirre his frozen spright' (23.4–5) – and some innuendoes are unwittingly perpetrated by Florimell herself, such as her advice to the old fisherman about controlling his 'cock-bote' in 24.4. Ironically, too, Florimell addresses as 'father' and 'good man' (23.7, 24.1) the old man who will in a couple of stanzas try roughly to grope her and will throw her on the floor of his boat. But in the rescue from the lecherous fisherman by Proteus she has simply ironically 'chaung'd from one to other feare' (viii 33.2). She is taken to Proteus's bower, where she will remain imprisoned until the final stanzas of Book IV, there to be further plagued with his sexual advances and terrified by his amatory shape-changing (viii 36–43). Eventually Florimell's only alternatives at the hands of men in Book III are loss of chastity or imprisonment. One could say that this is comically the logical result of her unwarranted (and neurotic?) fears about the male in Book III. After all, isn't Florimell's fear of men indiscriminate and undiscriminating? She feared the noble Arthur (unfairly?) as 'feend of hell' (iv 47.9) and his attempt to comfort her simply increased the speed of her flight. But maybe she was right and Arthur is more Ariostan in his pursuit than we think. What is the 'suit' and 'the hope/Of his long labour' Arthur so reluctantly abandons when he loses Florimell (iv 52)? Or perhaps the poem depicts her range of experience as claustrophobically limited and leaves her with such confined alternatives to demonstrate grotesquely the narrow range of options available to this vulnerable manifestation of the female in Book III. Sadly for Florimell, to be chaste is to be chased. The simple pun is even easier in sixteenth-century spelling (as illustrated, for instance, by 'And chaste so fiercely after fearefull flight', II x 16.5).

The flight of Florimell is one of Spenser's *imitations* of Ariosto's romance. Imitation was the practice, much approved of in the Renaissance, in which a literary work would model itself, often as an expression of admiration, on an eminent predecessor. The imitation should not be servile copying, but should be a remoulding. According to Petrarch, the imitator should

> take care that what he writes resembles the original without reproducing it precisely. The resemblance should not be that of a portrait to the sitter ... but of a son to his father ...[7]

Book III imitates at its beginning and then elaborates the flight of Ariosto's beautiful Angelica at the beginning of *Orlando Furioso*,

Canto i. You may wish to read the opening canto of Ariosto's poem to get a general impression of a Renaissance Italian romance and so be able to sense the differences between Ariosto and Spenser.[8]

We have seen that in Book I Spenser wrote a chivalric romance at least in part in imitation of Scripture, and in Book II a chivalric romance in imitation of parts of an epic from classical antiquity. In Book III his main model for his chivalric romance is another chivalric romance. Book I is the romance of Scripture (the text on which it bases itself is the New Testament, particularly the Apocalypse), Book II the romance of classical epic (the text on which it bases itself is the *Odyssey*), and Book III the romance of romance (the text on which it bases itself is Ariosto's *Orlando Furioso*). The previous books of the poem imitated distinctly different sorts of text (Scripture, classical epic); Book III is imitating something remarkably like itself.

Hence, the intertextuality of Book III is particularly dense and complex. In Chapter 5 (pp. 73–6) I suggested some reasons why I thought the poem requires an increasingly sophisticated reading of allegory as it progresses. We have already seen the complicated narrative technique and point of view in Book III. By the time we reach Book III reading is an increasingly complex relation of figures and texts. We read the internal relations of narratives and figures within Book III, the relation of Book III as a stratum of the poem to the strata of the previous two books, and the intertextual relation of Book III to texts external to Spenser's poem, one of which you have sampled in this chapter and others which we will look at in the next chapter.

Ariosto's chivalric romance, *Orlando Furioso*, whose opening lines promise to sing of 'Ladies, knights, war and love' was dedicated to and celebrates the aristocratic Este family of Ferrara, as Spenser's romance was dedicated to Elizabeth. There are actually moments we have looked at in previous books where Spenser has borrowed something from Ariosto: the story of Fradubio (I ii), Phedon's story (II iv), and details of Acrasia's garden (II xii) are some examples. Book III's imitation of Ariosto's poem is more extended and extensive, and as a result the character of this book is more intensely that of the 'romance'. This is a word that has been used generally of Spenser's poem in this and previous chapters of this *Guide*. The difficulty of defining it precisely is rehearsed later in this chapter. Although a combination of the relation of 'improbable adventures of idealized characters in some remote or enchanted setting',[9] together with the opening lines of Ariosto's *Orlando Furioso*, 'Ladies, knights, war and love', may

serve as a working definition, I think that this is the opportunity
to consider it more carefully.

One way of thinking of the distinctive character of Book III is
as the most 'romantic' of the books of the *Faerie Queene* you have
read so far, and perhaps the most 'romantic' of all the books of
the poem (Book VI is its rival). Spenser's poem is open to many
descriptions: allegory and heroic poem are two we have been
thinking about, 'romance' is another. But since 'all fiction has a
way of looking like romance... There is no single characteristic
which distinguishes the romance from other literary kinds',[10] and
'romance' could be used to describe works as diverse in kind and
distant in time as the *Odyssey* and *Return of the Jedi*, we will have
to focus our thinking more narrowly. As ever, investigation of the
noun (and verb) in the dictionary is revealing, and you might care
to do some reading about romance,[11] but I would suggest that a
useful way of considering romance in *Faerie Queene*, Book III, is
to see it in conjunction with Shakespeare's comedies. The history
and development of romance in Western literary culture has
many layers, rather like geological strata sedimented in the earth.
Shakespeare's comedies, although of course different in genre, are
contemporary with the publication of Spenser's poem and therefore at that moment in the late sixteenth and early seventeenth
centuries both display the same, most recent layers of the strata
of romance. Indeed, the main sources of almost all Shakespeare's
comedies, early, middle and late, are prose romances. The same
romance story of a lover's doubting of his lady's honour, vil-
lainously caused, is told in *Much Ado About Nothing*, *Faerie
Queene* (II iv), and *Orlando Furioso* (Canto v). And I think that
so many moments in *Faerie Queene*, Book VI, are like those in
Shakespeare's last comedies, such as *The Winter's Tale* and *The
Tempest*, that Shakespeare must have been one of the acutest
readers of the romance of the Book of Courtesy.

**From what you know of Shakespeare's comedies you may have
seen or read, what similarities do you think there are in incident,
situation, narrative, event, or preoccupation between the comedies
and *Faerie Queene*, Book III?**

DISCUSSION

Most obvious, I think, are their concern with love and courtship,
and their idealization of love and desire. Although there may be
moments when we see couples less high-minded and scrupulous
than the romance heroine and hero (look at the different sorts of

low comedy in the story of Hellenore and Paridell, III ix–x), romantic love is a noble and virtuous passion that promises the eventual finding of and union with an ideal other. Such a finding and union is the hope and end of the search of the various lovers for each other in Book III. Even the fleeing Florimell, we learn from her dwarf, is also questing for Marinell (v 10). I asked earlier in this chapter, what the quest of the knight of chastity is and whether she achieves it. The answers must be, I think, Artegall and not in Book III. For in romance 'the course of true love never did run smooth' (*A Midsummer Night's Dream*, I i 132), and 'journeys end in lovers meeting' only after a protracted period of separation or difficulty, misunderstanding and adversity which actually constitutes the narrative of romance, Spenser's legend of chastity and the dramatic action of romantic comedies. Britomart has a long search for Artegall, whom she and we only see in Book III as an image in a magic mirror and hear of in Redcrosse's praise (III ii). They will not meet until she will unknowingly unseat him in a joust in IV iv, and they finally recognize each other in a fight in IV vi. In Book V the poem delays their union and troubles their relationship, for romance tends to improvise numerous obstacles that love and lovers must overcome before the promised happy ending. Its deferral of a happy ending creates a narrative space and 'there begins new matter' for its stories. So as romance gets more romantic, its stories tend to proliferate, divide, digress and become more complicated. Gilbert Highet's characterization of the love entanglements of Renaissance pastoral drama serves equally well for romance: 'A loves B, B loves C, C loves D, and D is vowed to chastity'.[12] The multiple love entanglements and changing love pairings of *As You Like It* provide a useful comparison with what I have called 'polyphony' in narrative and with the mutiple points of view in Book III. *As You Like It* is a good example of a romantic comedy where 'in diuerse minds,/How diuersly loue doth his pageants play' (III v 1.1–2).

But if in romance we find idealization of love and desire, we can also see it causes pain, distress and longing, which all lovers in Book III suffer. It even allows in its margins glimpses of treachery, vanity and brutal desire (more so in Shakespeare's problem and late comedies). That is why the legend of chastity includes such figures as Hellenore, Argante and the old fisherman.

Both Shakespeare's comedies and the legend of chastity map the difficult transition from virginity to chaste sexual experience, which is usually ideally promised in a marriage that will take place after the action of the comedy ends. Marriage is one of the forms of union that the *Faerie Queene* defers until after Book III. It is rare in early or middle Shakespearian comedy that we see lovers after they are married (*All's Well That Ends Well* is an exception). This transition is effected through the first confused and confusing negotiations of young heterosexual couples we call falling in love, and through the rites of passage of courtship.

Other stock features, situations and motifs of Shakespeare's comedies which come to mind are wooing, flight, separation, cross-dressing, discussions of love, disguise, misunderstandings, and parallelism in relationships. There is often an education in love and self-discovery of various kinds for the heroine. Can you think of a few examples in *Faerie Queene*, Book III?

DISCUSSION

Britomart provides us with many of these, especially, I think, the last two. Like a number of Shakespearian heroines she adopts male dress. Britomart and Glauce contemplate the male disguising of Britomart in almost exactly the same language as Rosalind and Celia consider Rosalind's (III iii 53; *As You Like It*, I iii 106ff). This gives the woman power but also causes complicated mis-understandings. Britomart's disguise as male knight can produce a sort of in-joke with us as readers about an ironical situation or even a one-line equivocation ('Love haue I sure, (quoth she) but Lady none', i 28.2). Shakespeare's heroines disguised as boys can do the same with us as audience (see, for example, *Twelfth Night*, II iv 23–7, III i 43–7). The misunderstanding in the castle of Malecasta (III i) is like a low-comedy version of Olivia's passion for Cesario (Viola) in *Twelfth Night* (see *Twelfth Night*, III). Cross-dressing has its disadvantages, as Rosalind disguised as a boy discovers when her lover Orlando comes to Arden: 'Alas the day, what shall I do with my doublet and hose?' (*As You Like It*, III ii 12–13) and can cause its moments of isolation. Viola's intro-spective musings about her grief and situation offer an interesting comparison with Britomart's predicament in Malecasta's castle. Both she and Viola are conscious of the irony of being wooed by a woman while they are suffering the pangs of love for a man, and indeed consequently have some sympathy for their wooers (look especially at *Faerie Queene*, III i 53–54).

To conclude this chapter please consider the following passage on romance. Gillian Beer, instead of providing a definition of this appropriately diffuse term, suggests 'a cluster of properties' as characterising the romance:

> the themes of love and adventure, a certain withdrawal from their own societies on the part of both reader and romance hero, profuse

sensuous detail, simplified characters (often with a suggestion of allegorical significance), a serene intermingling of the unexpected and the everyday, a complex and prolonged succession of incidents usually without a single climax, a happy ending, amplitude of proportions, a strongly enforced code of conduct to which all the characters must comply.[13]

As a way of consolidating your work on romance and on Book III, and also as a way of marshalling in your memory some of its numerous incidents, consider whether Beer's 'properties' are properties of Book III. Are they all to be found there? Which best describe your experience of Book III?

8. 'Endlesse Worke'

'But yet the end is not. There *Merlin* stayd,...'

                                (*Faerie Queene*, III iii 50.1)

In Chapter 7 I asked you to look particularly at Florimell, and we also looked at Britomart looking at Florimell at the beginning of Book III. We will start this chapter by looking at Britomart looking at something else, a series of tapestries. **Please read closely i 34–38.** These stanzas are an example of *ecphrasis*, a description of a work of art in a literary text. You have encountered in passing at least one previous example of Spenserian ecphrasis in the ivory gate to Acrasia's garden which tells parts of the quest story of Jason (II xii 43–45). The one at III i 34–38 tells the Ovidian story of Venus and Adonis (*Metamorphoses*, X 519–739) which is also the subject of a narrative poem, *Venus and Adonis*, by Shakespeare. Ideally, you should also read the brief story of Venus and Adonis in Ovid and think about how he tells the story. As with so many classical myths, Ovid's was the most influential version for Western literature.

I think that there is a series of tapestries here, as there often were in great Renaissance houses. It is difficult to be sure exactly how many, but I think at least three: 'First' (34.7ff), 'Then' (35.1ff), and finally 'Lo' (38.1). **What are the events of the story depicted in the tapestries? How is the story treated in the tapestries? From whose point of view?**

DISCUSSION

Stanza 34 announces a tale of love and transformation. First Venus, desiring Adonis's beauty, suffers the pangs and bitter pains of love. Stanza 35 shows her skilfully courting him, decking and leading him to a bower, bathing him and putting him to sleep. In stanza 36 she watches Adonis sleeping. Stanza 37 depicts her enjoyment of him and her advice against hunting the boar. Stanza 38 dramatically depicts the dying Adonis gored by the boar, shows his wound and his final transformation into a flower.

I find it much easier to identify the point of view than how the story is treated. Clearly the point of view is Venus's (as it is in Shakespeare's poem). The tapestries show the progress of a love affair with the female partner dominant and initiatory. The tapestries certainly show the sufferings of love, but there is something that makes one uneasy about the way that they depict the relationship. Don't you think Venus infantilizes Adonis with her bathing and tucking-up? I also feel that there is something voyeuristic in stanza 36 as Venus views Adonis's body with her 'two crafty spyes' (36.5). The tone of some scenes, in the secret central concealment of a bower, feels like a hangover from Acrasia's garden. This representation of Venus and Adonis recalls Acrasia feeding off Verdant (look again at II xii 73). I think that my impression is of a myth somehow improperly represented.

Britomart here is looking at a tapestry version of a myth which provides a sort of 'programme' for many of the experiences of love in Book III. In Chapter 7 we saw how romance accounted for some of Beer's 'cluster of properties' of Book III. **What are those moments where you find the story of Venus and Adonis manifesting itself in Book III, either through direct allusion, or indirectly in its incidents and motifs?**

DISCUSSION

The experiences of Venus and Adonis provide a paradigm for the typical experiences of the pains of love in the legend of chastity: the tender heart smitten with beauty, the female sufferings caused by love presented in their different varieties in Britomart, Florimell and Amoret. We looked at love and hunting (and their similarities) in Chapter 7.

Adonis displays the wound of love, a constant motif suffered by both men and women in Book III. In the discussions in Chapter 7, relationships between the sexes in Book III seemed to be emerge as flight, separation, division, and confinement. This myth has motifs of wounding, aggression and pain. Britomart is multiply wounded: in the first canto by Gardante (i 65), and again in the last by Busirane, who also brought about Amoret's painfully exposed wound. The bleeding wound of love is often used as a metaphor, as in the case of Malecasta (i 56.3). The wounded Adonis gored by the boar (Spenser does not tell us, but Ovid says Adonis was wounded in the groin) anticipates other wounded male lovers: Marinell (in the left side where the heart is, iv 16) and Timias (in the left thigh, v 20). Malecasta is a burlesque Venus almost instantly inflamed with the love of a young man (Britomart), and the first tapestry is re-enacted in her castle, where the costliness of the tapestry is replicated in her court. Malecasta is also, like Venus, an active wooer and experienced in the arts and deceits of love.

The myth which is the subject of Malecasta's tapestry most obviously reappears again elaborated in the middle of Book III in Venus's Garden of Adonis. This garden occupies a large section of Canto vi, reproposes problems of mortality and transience integral to the myth, and attempts to answer them. The tapestries show Adonis beautiful, youthful and mortal, Venus immortal. The very flowers with which she decks him are symbols of transience (look back at the rose song in Acrasia's garden, II xii 64–75) but his metamorphosis into a flower is also a way of evading death. The tapestries show Adonis dying and wounded, but not dead, the present participle 'languishing' (38.1) lingeringly preserves life. The moment of Adonis's death is actually elided, we see him not dead but only dying or transformed. In both the tapestry and the Garden of Adonis the lovers consummate their passion, unlike most other characters in this book.

Malecasta's Ovidian tapestries also look forward to similarly Ovidian tapestries in the House of Busirane which tell of the transformation and desires of gods and mortals.

I have been asking you to think about the tapestries' content, their treatment of that content and the relevance to other parts of the legend of chastity. I would now like to turn to ecphrasis itself.

In Chapter 7 I suggested the curious way in which Book III turns inward to reflect on itself: in imitating Ariosto it romances

romance and hence imitates something like itself, and extraordinarily Britomart seems able to read the allegorical significance
of an episode in which she is a figure. So also ecphrases in
literature (there are famous ones in classical epics) tend to dwell
self-reflexively on their own peculiar medium. By depicting a work
of art, usually a picture of some sort, in words, ecphrasis invites
reflection on the relationship between words and pictures, how
the two media operate and how pictures are put into words. It
implicitly draws its reader's attention to the fact that this imagined
visual work of art is actually a textual production, a creation in
words. Reflection on a picture tends to extend to reflection on
the text and the artistry which produced that text. Ecphrases
often draw explicit attention to the skill of their craftsmanship
and hence that of the craftsman ('cunning hand...A worke of
rare deuice, and wondrous wit', III i 34.3–6). Ecphrasis appears
merely to be describing a work of art, but actually creates a work
of art which only has existence in the text. Keats's poem 'Ode on
a Grecian Urn' is a good and a very complex example of this
process. The tapestries in the House of Busirane present ecphrases
at the opposite end of the book from those in Malecasta's castle.
In between there are descriptions of other works of art which,
although not strictly ecphrases, also strike us by their pictorial
quality, and the formality and ingenuity of their construction: the
false Florimell and the Masque of Cupid. The masque was the
most formally picture-like of Renaissance dramatic forms.

**With Book III's concern with its own artistry in mind, consider
the five stanzas which are the Proem right at the beginning of
Book III. What is the poet's concern here and how does he think
of his work as a writer?**

DISCUSSION

The poet contemplates his task in Book III of writing of chastity.
This task is constantly imaged as that of a painter. Elizabeth will
provide an 'ensample' (1.4) and her heart a 'pourtraict' (1.8) of
chastity, if any art *can* portray it. Great attention was paid in Elizabeth's reign to how the queen was painted, as the exact terms
of her representation involved important political issues. The poet
may even be imagining himself as painting chastity's portrait. He
cites the cases of classical artists (2.3), refers to the paints and
brushes of the painter's trade ('pencill' in 2.2 probably means a
miniaturist's brush) and sets up the same sort of dialogue between
visual and textual representation which we have seen initiated

by an ecphrasis. The Proem, too, shares what is apparently the book's intense and self-reflexive interest in its own modes of representation. It is also concerned with beauty (note that chastity's excellence is expressed as it being the *fairest* virtue) and its depiction, and we only have to turn the poem back literally one page in the Penguin edition to recall what a lively and problematic issue this was in Acrasia's garden.

With these issues in mind I'd like to take you back for a moment to representations of Florimell. In examining III i 14–20 we examined the initial presentation of her beauty and also Britomart's allegorical perception of Florimell's pursuit as 'beauties chace'. One of the many consequences of her flight and her provocation of male desire is the witch's manufacture of a duplicate Florimell to satisfy her son. **Consider the description of this other Florimell in III viii 5–9, in relation to two brief extracts, the first from Petrarch's description of his memory of the first sight of his mistress's head and face, the second from praise of his mistress by the Elizabethan poet, Thomas Watson. What do you think of the language used to represent feminine beauty in all these cases? Then consider how the description of the false Florimell differs from that we have already considered of the real one (i 15–16). Can we restrospectively use the false Florimell to 'read' the real one? How do we tell them apart, something that characters in the poem by and large find impossible to do in Books III and IV ('many it mistooke', III viii 5.9).**

> Her head refined gold, her face warm snow,
> Her eyebrows ebony, her eyes two stars
> From which Love's bow did not miss its mark;
> Pearls and vermilion roses, where gathered
> Grief shaped burning and beautiful words;
> Her sighs were flames of fire, crystal her tears.[1]
>
> Hark you that list to hear what saint I serve:
> Her yellow locks exceed the beaten gold;
> Her sparkling eyes in heaven a place deserve;
> Her forehead high and fair of comely mould;
> . . .
> On either cheek a Rose and Lily lies;
> Her breath is sweet perfume, or holy flame;
> Her lips more red than any coral stone.[2]

DISCUSSION

These extracts are from two 'blasons', conventional catalogue descriptions of the admirable physical features of the poet's lady.

In all cases, including the false Florimell, I think that the language strikes us as artificial. Live beauty is often compared to inanimate objects. The false Florimell shares with her sisters specifically composition from snow, 'vermily' (viii 6.8), and hair made of gold. More generally, she is made up from the substance of materials which in Petrarch and Watson are metaphors or similes for feminine beauty. In the poem's fiction the witch 'literally' does by magic what Petrarchist poets do metaphorically. Spenser is very self-consciously 'constructing' this Florimell from conventional poetic metaphors for beauty from the poems of his contemporaries. (You might also look at Shakespeare's ironic treatment of these comparisons in sonnet 130: 'My mistress' eyes are nothing like the sun'). As in Malecasta's tapestries, attention is again drawn to craftsmanship in construction. The emphasis in viii 5 is on the *manufacture* of another Florimell and the ingenious craftsmanship exerted (wit, deviz'd, frame, framed, counterfeit, make).

I find the question about the relation and distinction between the true and false Florimell much harder to answer, which is perhaps a sign of the fineness of distinctions made in Book III and its increasingly discriminating allegorical perceptions. Does the manufactured Florimell differ so much from her original with her face like crystal or whalebone, her long golden hair and her garments of beaten gold? Look how many of these details are also in Petrarch and Watson. And the false Florimell apparently replicates the real one's aversion to sexual advances, her valuing of her chaste honour, and her fearfulness (viii 14–15). I am inclined to see the false Florimell as exaggerating to a grotesque and inert degree, and thus making far more obvious, certain traits observable in the true one. She reveals artificiality, even the obviousness of Florimell's conventional beauty (fairy-tale princess), a beauty unanimously registered by characters in this book ('the fairest wight aliue' v 5.9). The exaggeration also makes clearer the ease with which male poetic conventional description and figurative language can falsify and make dolls out of women. The false duplicate points to something unsatisfactory, perhaps not so much about the virtues or merits of the 'character' Florimell, as allegorically about the perception, construction and desire of beauty at this moment in Book III.

I'd now like further to complicate and refine these issues and, incidentally, engage you in reading with the accumulating sense of the way that some of these same poetic conventions are used by the poet to construct Belphoebe's beauty in her long portrait in Book II. **Aren't they used 'straight' at II iii 21–30? If we compare**

the false Florimell and Belphoebe, are we to make a distinction
which is favourable to Belphoebe, and if so, how and why?

DISCUSSION

Belphoebe's description uses some formulae which seem exactly
like those in the make-up of the false Florimell: Belphoebe's
cheeks, too, are 'vermeill red' and are like roses and lilies, her eyes
are flaming lamps (22–23), her hair like golden wire (30), let
alone the elaborate general artifice in the depiction of the rest of
her body. Can we say that the poet has freshly animated conventional description in the elaborate and fresh vitality of his
beautiful virgin Belphoebe, as opposed to the deadness of the
manufactured, lifeless thing which is the false Florimell who 'in
the stead/Of life' has a spirit animating a dead machine of a
carcase? The 'it' (rather than 'her') is telling in III viii 5.9. The
spirit rolls the eyes in the sockets of false Florimell's head like a
doll's.

Finally, another interrelation between different books of the
Faerie Queene. Think back to Archimago's making of the false
Una in I i and our examination of this moment in Chapter 3.
What relations do you think there might be between the witch's
manufacture of the false Florimell and Archimago's of the false
Una, and what is their significance?

DISCUSSION

I suggested in Chapter 3 that part of the significance of the false
Una was its false likeness, and hence allegorically its misrepresentation of truth. The false duplicate was representation
detached from what it should represent. In I i we saw the 'artes',
'witt' and 'guile' of Archimago's artifice as a 'maker', and the
sixteenth-century use of that term for 'poet' led me to say that the
magician's art is analogous to the poet's: both may deceive in their
representations. I think that something similar is the case with the
witch's manufacture of the snowy lady. In both instances magic
fabricates a false female representation and our attention is drawn
to the maker's art. There are verbal echoes, too: False Una was 'So
liuely, and so like in all mens sight' (I i 45.4), False Florimell is
similarly 'So liuely and so like' (III viii 5.9). In both artefacts there
is a sense of representation without meaning, and of emptied and
untruthful representation. Both are false replications of the real
thing.

The false Una soon disappeared from the poem although

perhaps only to give way to another false duplication in Duessa. The false Florimell's admittedly unstable constitution from snow, mercury and wax is yet slightly more substantial than the airy body of false Una, and it has staying power to last, deceive and confuse. The distinction between the true and false Una was clear to us, even if it was not to Redcrosse. The witch's son's extreme joy at being given the Spenserian equivalent of an inflatable doll comments on his lack of discrimination and how easily he is pleased ('Enough to hold a foole in vaine delight', III viii 10.7). But one ought not to single out the witch's son for contempt. The boastful Braggadocchio finds the snowy lady worth taking from the witch's son, and a unnamed knight takes her in turn from Braggadocchio. She will be able to deceive a whole series of worthier knights in Books IV and V. She will at last be placed side by side with the real Florimell and melt in V iii. Both Archimago's and the witch's puppets are false fabrications wrought by magic. Both may be read as literary allegories about the possible falseness of poetic fabrication, a counterfeit replication of, respectively, truth and beauty, in what Shakespeare in Sonnet 130 calls 'false compare'.

I want to keep the focus on Book III's literary self-awareness and turn to a scene involving Britomart in Canto iv. For the best part of two cantos the poet has been telling us of the origins of Britomart's love for Artegall. She parts from Redcrosse in iv 4, and 5–6 describe her increasing isolation and introspection, and the growth of the wound of love which she nourishes by her introspection and imaginings. **Please read III iv 6–11 in conjunction with the poem reproduced below.** It is a sonnet by the sixteenth-century English poet, Sir Thomas Wyatt, and is one of a number of love poems in the sixteenth century which imitate an Italian love-sonnet by Petrarch[3] in which is elaborated a *conceit* of a ship. Spenser himself wrote one in his collection of sonnets, *Amoretti* (*Amoretti*, XXIV), which you would find a further interesting comparision. A conceit is very like allegory as trope in that it is an elaborate metaphor or simile which asserts similarity between two dissimilar things, in a way which we might think fanciful.

My galley charged with forgetfulness
Thorough sharp seas in winter nights doth pass
'Tween rock and rock; and eke my enemy, alas,
That is my lord, steereth with cruelness;
And every oar a thought in readiness
As though that death were light in such a case.
An endless wind doth tear the sail apace

Of forced sighs and trusty fearfulness.
A rain of tears, a cloud of dark disdain
Hath done the wearied cords great hindrance,
Wreathed with error and eke with ignorance.
The stars be hid that led me to this pain.
Drowned is reason that should me comfort
And I remain despairing of the port.[4]

This is yet another of Britomart's many 'speculations' in Book III, one of those moments (like her looking at Merlin's mirror in Canto ii, or Busirane's tapestries or the Masque of Cupid in Cantos xi–xii) where the poem has her look at something. **What is Britomart's relation to her surroundings and what she sees here, and what are their relevance to her? What part does she play in constructing what she sees? What sorts of 'literary self-awareness' does this passage show?**

DISCUSSION

In iv 7 Britomart sat down on the rocky sea-shore and 'complaynd' (7.9), that is, technically delivered a certain sort of love lament, of which Wyatt's poem is an example. Now we might say that Britomart has been brought dramatically to a location which gives her the opportunity, stimulus and appropriate background to express her love-grief. The same is true allegorically. Just as Redcrosse's despair brought him to the wasted landscape around the Cave of Despair (I ix), so the inner tumult of Britomart's love brings her to a sight of the roaring sea. We could say, as Spenser does, that love brings her here (6.8), but he also says in the next line that the choice of direction was hers. The remarkable thing is, I think, that one could say that Britomart is aware of the allegorical implications of this moment in the poem, as I suggested she was when she watched 'beauties chace' in III i. Not only does she again voice the allegorical meaning of her surroundings, here it is she who *constructs* them, as it is she who names the sea's significance as sorrow and grief (8.1). She first imposes her inner state on her external landscape and then, at the end of iv 8, internalizes the landscape on her inner emotional state. Britomart's remarkable and self-conscious allegorization of her landscape and her situation in it merges with the poet's allegorical decision to place her in this landscape to make visible the troubled condition of love in Book III. Britomart, I would say, is actually writing allegory as allegory writes her. Some critics claim that in the 'dizzying but creative self-consciousness of *Hamlet*'[5] Hamlet seems to be conscious of himself as a character in a revenge play.

Similarly, not only does the consciousness of Britomart, more than of any other previous character in the poem, seem akin to that of the reader of an allegorical poem, but also she seems to possess the ability to *write* allegory. Stanza 7 almost sees her as composing herself to deliver the signification of her topography, and then she finishes off this passage almost like closing up a book: 'She shut vp all her plaint' (iv 11.2). Britomart's complaint was already recognized as a sort of allegory by Alexander Gil in 1619.[6]

Britomart has taken the internal landscape of the conceit in Wyatt's poem and incorporated it into an allegorical writing of her surroundings. A comparison with Wyatt's poem confirms this sense of self-conscious allegorical fashioning. Britomart at this moment seems to be writing the poem which is writing her. Looking back to Book II, I would even say that Britomart wittily appropriates and refashions in the service of chaste desire one of the important images in the allegory of temperance. She refashions the figure of the ship from Guyon's journey in II xii. There the pilot and boatswain signified reason and effort: Britomart rewrites them to represent love as a pilot and fortune as boatswain (iv 9). Britomart has appropriated and refashioned an allegorical trope from elsewhere in the poem.

Our treatment of Book III in this chapter and in Chapter 7 has so far been concerned largely with two female figures and the self-conscious awareness of representation in Book III. I want finally to turn to representation and women, and repose some questions which have been arising ever since the end of Chapter 3 (pp. 45–7). There I asked very general feminist questions of the poem which we would have to re-examine as we read further into the poem.

Can we consider Book III of the *Faerie Queene* a 'feminist' text? And is it 'feminist' not only in the sense that it lends itself to feminist analyses, but also in the sense that it participates in the Renaissance *questione delle donne* (the Renaissance, too, debated 'the woman question') and does so on the side of women? We might also ask this question of the first two books of the poem. These are large questions and you must not think that it is possible to answer them immediately, and certainly not before this *Guide* ends in a few pages. **Bearing the larger questions in mind, try addressing a series of smaller ones. First, the question of readership. The whole poem is dedicated to Elizabeth I. Does Book III have any special appeal to her? And is there evidence for a particular address to female readers? What evidence is there in Book III of women as implied readers?** I expect that you have noticed that often the poet turns to his audience in the first stanza of a new canto and addresses them on various subjects. What evidence is offered in the first stanzas of cantos in Book III?

DISCUSSION

You will already have noticed the particular address to Elizabeth when I directed you to the Proem on a different subject. There the virtue of chastity is described as especially enshrined in the queen. And surely in the Proem, too, women are implied as readers who can look at and read the virtue of chastity written in Elizabeth, and then in the chaste Elizabeth as she is particularly written in Gloriana and Belphoebe (see stanza 5 of the Proem). In Book III generally, Britomart's story also provides Elizabeth with a glorious ancestry, for its fiction looks forward to and legitimizes her reign as destined by providence.

The opening stanzas of cantos often address women or topics of interest to them. The first two stanzas of III ii blame men for neglecting the memory of female chivalry, and the queen is directly addressed in ii 3. The first two stanzas of III iv return to the subject of the achievements of women in history, and vi 1 addresses 'faire Ladies' on the subject of Belphoebe. There are also many other addresses and asides to female readers – for example, at i 49, provoked by the behaviour of Malecasta, and at ix 1, apologizing in advance for writing of Hellenore, a 'wanton Lady'. This last stanza appears even-handedly to address knights *and* ladies 'To whom I leuell all my labours end'. It apologizes for being about to write of a wanton lady, as well as of a 'faithlesse knight'. The carefully balanced patterning of words in this stanza (knights, dames, wanton lady, faithless knight), rhetorically exemplifies its even-handedness. All this, I think, is evidence for the book's particular address to women readers.

And what of the content of Book III? How much is it concerned with women and their relationships? Does it give prominence and importance to women?

DISCUSSION

Quite obviously women are prominent in Book III. Even the Angles are made to call themselves after the female warrior, Angela (iii 56.7). These two chapters which have concentrated on Florimell and Britomart are themselves a tribute to this. The book of chastity is thus dominated by the narratives of female characters: Britomart, Florimell and Amoret are the main ones.

And the powerful and beautiful virgin and huntress, Belphoebe, returns to the narrative after a long absence. As a huntress she reverses the pattern of the male hunt of love (note that at v 28 the beast she hunts is associated with Timias). The book's presiding deity is female, Venus the goddess of love, who actually appears in the course of the poet's story explaining the birth of Amoret and Belphoebe. We hear most of Britomart, Florimell and their intertwined narratives, although interestingly they never meet. The legend of chastity is also concerned with relationships between women – for example, the relationship of Britomart with her aged nurse Glauce is Book III's version of knight and squire. And surely it is the interrelationships of women which determine the allegory of Book III. When we looked at the 'polyphony' of Book III our attention was naturally directed to the polyphonic relations between Britomart and Amoret, and between Britomart, Florimell and the false Florimell. Although male figures and narratives have a contribution to make to the poetry, narrative and meaning of Book III, its significance is primarily constituted by female figures and signs, and stories of female relationships. Glauce takes care of Britomart, Britomart takes care of Amoret (and indeed will protect her into Book IV) and only she is able to free Amoret from the House of Busirane.

In the context of this discussion I would like you now to look at what is usually considered as one of the book's most difficult cantos, III vi. I am not going to concentrate on the usual question here, which is the meaning of Spenser's mythopoeia (myth-making) in the Garden of Adonis (vi 29–51). Instead, please consider the place of the whole canto as a piece of feminine mythopoeia.

DISCUSSION

I think that the evidence of III vi is especially important in discussions of feminist issues in Book III, although I am not entirely sure what conclusions to draw from this evidence. The canto's cast list is almost exclusively female, including two female deities. It is the story of a sort of virgin birth of female twins, without a father. The genealogy of Belphoebe is exclusively female (Amphisa, Chrysogonee, vi 4). In this canto, where the poet is at his most self-consciously mythopoeic in the poem so far, the myths provide feminine aetiologies (causes for things being as they are). They are myths of female generation and nurturing. Amoret is adopted by Venus and replaces the lost male son, Cupid. Cupid is seen later as a sadistic, cruel tyrant in the house of Busirane (xii 22–23).

Amoret is brought into her garden by Venus and entrusted to her daughter-in-law, Psyche, to be 'trained vp in true feminitee' (51.5). Of the first three books of the *Faerie Queene*, Spenser is thought to be at his most inventive and mythopoeic in Book III. It echoes ancient myths and archetypes; flight to the sea and imprisonment underneath it, the making of something that looks human (false Florimell), the garden, long-lasting wounds, ordeals in a mysterious castle. The inventive feminine mythopoeia of III vi matches the poet's own.

The canto also seems deliberately to use language and images derived from areas significantly feminine. Even the court is the 'schoolmistresse' (vi 1.6, not schoolmaster) of all courtesy, a word which apparently was first being used in English in the sixteenth century. The Garden of Adonis uses images of female sexual organs in its double gates (vi 31) and the Mount of Venus shaded with myrtle and dropping sweet gum (vi 43). Indeed, in the whole canto the emphasis is on female reproduction rather than male, at a time when the Renaissance cultural emphasis was still the Aristotelian idea of the woman as merely the seed-bed where the male planted the far more important seed. Whatever the detailed meanings of this canto, it is significantly placed in Book III. It is central, generative and feminine.

It seems to me, therefore, that there is a strong case for Book III as a whole to be seen as voicing in its language, incidents, figures and allegory, concerns that we could call feminist. Britomart (whose emotions are at one point described metaphorically as gestation, ii 11) is obviously an admirable and powerful female representation. She has the most elaborate personal and psychic history of any character yet in the poem, and even in her absence is a stable reference point in Book III. In her determined quest and progress she is a mean balanced between the extremes of Florimell, the woman in constant, agitated flight from men, and Amoret, the woman immobile, chained and imprisoned by a man in the House of Busirane. Indeed, these extremes collapse into each other when Florimell's flight ends in an incarceration, like Amoret's, by a magician.

But perhaps you may think that Britomart's superiority as a female representation is at the expense of Florimell or Amoret. Rereading Chapter 7, I was struck by the way I seem to be implying that Florimell caused and therefore actually deserved her problems. To my own disquiet, I found there were moments when I seem to be implying that it is Florimell's *fault* that she is pursued by men. This was certainly not my (conscious) intention, but perhaps I exposed either my unconscious feeling or that of the text. And what is the contribution of Cantos ix–x to our discussion of the representation of women? What about the depiction of Hellenore? Does ix 2 satisfactorily answer the problems it raises? And is Britomart's chaste white to be seen shining all the brighter against Hellenore's black? Britomart's imagination is fired by history, heroism and tragedy; Hellenore's by lewd lore, secrets, and the cryptic game of love.

As I said earlier, these are complex and difficult questions and there is no easy answer to them. **Let me ask you again: if Book III is feminist, is it the exception among the first three?**

DISCUSSION

On this question I can only venture a provisional opinion. It seems to me that Book III represents a superior state which, to use a very Spenserian word, 'overgoes'[7] (overtakes, surpasses) the two previous books and towards which they are working. I suggested in Chapter 5 that Spenser's allegory proceeds in geometric rather than arithmetical progression. We may reasonably expect that Book III will build on Book II as Book II did on Book I. This seems true in the increased sophistication it demands in reading, the increased complexity of its narratives and available points of view, and the sophistication it manifests in the consciousness of its female knight. In the previous chapter we have seen the extraordinary specularity that is suddenly manifested in Britomart as reader.

In retrospect from Book III, we might wish to say that in terms of chastity, the 'fairest vertue, farre aboue the rest' (Proem 1.2), both the knights of holiness and temperance were lacking and underdeveloped. Redcrosse was notably deficient, Guyon excessively rigorous. Book III expresses such a view by having the knight of chastity 'overthrow' a rather intemperately rash and wrathful knight of temperance at its opening. Perhaps Book III wittily develops Book II's notion of the ideal of the mean and manifests it in Britomart.

Consider, finally, the two endings of Book III. Its ending in the first edition of the *Faerie Queene* (1590), comprising only the first three books which we have been considering, is numbered in the Penguin edition III xii 43a–47a (pp. 561–2). First reread these and then reread III xii 43–45 (pp. 560–1) which was the ending in the 1596 edition containing Books I–VI of the poem. What difference to the sense of an ending to Book III does the change make? The 1590 union of Amoret and Scudamour is the last

image in Book III seen by Britomart, who has spent so much of
Book III as a reader of sights and images. Why, do you think, does
Spenser use the image of the hermaphrodite (xii 46a) to describe
the union of Scudamour and Amoret in the 1590 version?

DISCUSSION

Clearly the 1590 version gives a more conclusive 'end' to Book III
and provides a reunion for at least one pair of its divided and
suffering lovers. The embrace and physical melting and union of
the lovers extends the notion of the closing of the wound of love
and separated lovers, so painfully incarnate in Amoret's body in
the House of Busirane. Stanza 45a describes the bliss of Amoret
and Scudamour, and stanza 46a images them as the statue of a
hermaphrodite, the last example of the book's interest in artistic
objects and their representation of love. The hermaphrodite, combining both sexes in one body, had long been an image of union
and perfection, especially in love, since a famous early use of it in
Plato's dialogue on love, the *Symposium*. But even in 1590 it is a
union that can only be watched, not experienced, by Britomart.
The 1596 version postpones even the one reunion of Amoret and
Scudamour and seems intent on continuing the wide dispersal of
characters in Book III: Britomart returns with Amoret to find not
only Scudamour gone but also Glauce. If the last stanza of the
1590 Book III looks forward to an imminent cessation of work
and to a holiday, 1596 offers in the last word of Book III only a
temporary catching of breath ('respire'). Quite clearly in 1596 we
are about to press on with our quest, with a still increasing
complexity and still in search of the poem's many ends and
unions.

It is at this point, with Book IV in prospect, that this book
must end. I hope that it has made you want to pursue the quest of
reading further into the *Faerie Queene*. The stories of the lovers
continue into Book IV. Britomart finally finds Artegall in Book V,
but only after she has dreamt of having sex with a crocodile and
has had to rescue Artegall from a formidable woman who has
dressed him in woman's clothes ... This is the Amazon Radegund
who bears a striking resemblance in some ways to Britomart
herself (and Elizabeth I?), and whose representation presents
fascinating issues for feminist interpretation. All this takes place
against the background of the Book of Justice, which has issues
topical for both Spenser's original readers and us in its treatment
of justice and foreign policy in Ireland. Book VI is the Book
of Courtesy, and sees the poem return eagerly to romance at its

end: lost daughters, shepherds, brigands, cannibals, a vison of the Graces dancing on a mountain, and one of Spenser's most wonderful and noisy monsters (it has a hundred tongues), the Blatant Beast.

The final version of the poem appeared in 1609, ten years after Spenser's death. This was a version which consisted of six completed books and two cantos and two stanzas which describe themselves as 'Two cantos of Mvtabilitie: which, both for forme and matter, appeare to be parcell of some following booke of the Faerie Qveene under the Legend of Constancie'. This heading poses some of the questions which arise about them. Are they part of the poem? If so, how? What part? What is (or would have been) the Legend of Constancie? These cantos are one of the Renaissance's moving meditations on change, and restate the discussion which cropped up in Book III in the Garden of Adonis. And the poem has one of the most tremendous endings (or non-endings?) in English poetry, although the last two stanzas are headed 'The VIII Canto, vnperfite' [unfinished]. At this point, as we 'respire' at the end(s) of Book III, I hope that you will wish to reach that other end, of the Mutabilitie cantos, or as some people, including myself, would wish to think of it, the perfect completion of the *Faerie Queene*, Book VII.

Notes and References

Chapter 1 – Beginnings

1 Jonathan Goldberg, *Endlesse Worke: Spenser and the structures of discourse* (Johns Hopkins University Press: Baltimore, MD 1981).

2 *The Faerie Queene* ed. A. C. Hamilton (Longman: London and New York 1977), p. 8.

3 Sir Richard Blackmore, 1695, in R. M. Cummings, ed., *Spenser: The Critical Heritage* (Routledge and Kegan Paul: London 1971), p. 226.

4 Unless otherwise indicated all translations are my own.

5 Aristotle, *Rhetoric*, 1404. An eminent Spenserian exclaims about his own use of language in writing about the Error episode, 'How difficult it is to avoid metaphor!', A. C. Hamilton, *The Structure of Allegory in the Faerie Queene* (Clarendon Press: Oxford 1961), p. 39. An interesting short discussion which touches on the issue of the distinction between figurative and non-figurative language is Thomas McLaughlin, 'Figurative Language' in Frank Lentricchia and Thomas McLaughlin, eds, *Critical Terms for Literary Study* (Chicago University Press: Chicago and London 1990), pp. 80–90.

6 Jonson, 'Timber: or Discoveries' in *Complete Poems*, ed. George Parfitt (Penguin: Harmondsworth, 1975), p. 428; Sidney, *An Apology for Poetry*, ed. Geoffrey Shepherd (Manchester University Press: Manchester, 1973), p. 133.

7 Spenser, *The Shepheardes Calender*, Epistle to Gabriel Harvey, in Spenser, *Poetical Works*, ed. J. C. Smith and E. de Selincourt (Oxford University Press: Oxford 1912), p. 417

8 Bacon, 'Of Studies' in *The Essays*, ed. John Pitcher (Penguin: Harmondsworth 1985), p. 209.

9 Ecclesiastes 12:12; the verse continues 'and much study is a weariness of the flesh'.

10 John M. Steadman, 'Error' in A. C. Hamilton, Donald Cheney, W. F. Blisset, David A. Richardson and William W. Barker, eds, *The Spenser Encyclopaedia* (University of Toronto Press: Toronto and Buffalo, and Routledge: London 1990), pp. 252–3; Douglas Brooks-

Davies, *Spenser's Faerie Queene: A Critical Commentary on Books I and II* (Manchester University Press: Manchester 1977), pp. 18–23; A. C. Hamilton, *The Structure of Allegory in The Faerie Queene* (Clarendon Press: Oxford 1961), pp. 30–43; John M. Steadman, 'Spenser's *Errour* and the Renaissance Allegorical Tradition', *Neuphilologische Mitteilungen*, 62 (1961), 22–38; James Nohrnberg, *The Analogy of the Faerie Queene* (Princeton University Press: Princeton, NJ 1976), pp. 135–51.

Chapter 2 – Reading and Allegory

1 Spenser, *The Faerie Queene*, ed. A. C. Hamilton (Longman: London and New York 1977), p. 18.

2 Ibid., p. 8.

3 This idea of intertextuality is particularly associated with the work in the late 1960s of Julia Kristeva, who coined the term.

4 *Allegoria est alieniloquium* [literally something like 'Allegory is other-speak'], Isidore of Seville, *Etymologies*, I.xxxvii.

5 The Geneva Bible was first printed complete at Geneva in 1560. It was the English Protestant family Bible and more popular than its rival, the Bishops' Bible (1568). It also came with more marginal notes and commentary than the Bishops', so we can read the simultaneous Protestant interpretations of the scriptural text in the marginal glosses. Unless otherwise indicated, it is used for all biblical quotations in this *Guide*, as it was the popular Protestant English translation read by Spenser and his contemporaries. I have used it also with the intention of defamiliarizing biblical texts for readers, so that passages may strike you freshly. You may find it interesting to compare its translations with those in the Authorised Version or modern translations of the Bible, and to reflect on the ways in which each different translation is itself necessarily an act of interpretation.

6 George Puttenham, *The Arte of English Poesie*, ed. Gladys Doidge Willcock and Alice Walker (Cambridge University Press: Cambridge 1936), p. 187.

7 Spenser, *The Faerie Queene*, ed. John Upton (1758), cited in *The Works of Spenser: A Variorum Edition*, ed. Edwin Greenlaw *et al.*, 11 vols (Johns Hopkins University Press: Baltimore, MD 1932–57), vol. 1, p. 176. Spenser himself explicitly acknowledges the analogue in the Letter to Ralegh: 'that is the armour of a Christian man specified by Saint Paul v. Ephes.', *The Faerie Queene*, (Penguin edition), p. 17.

8 In the Greek text of the Epistle the Greek word *kalymma* for 'veil' is here used in these verses uniquely in the New Testament.

9 F. D. E. Schleiermacher, 'The Hermeneutics: outline of the 1819 lectures', tr. Jan Wojcik and Roland Haas, *New Literary History*, 10 (1978), 1 cited by Joel Weinsheimer, 'Hermeneutics' in G. Douglas Atkins and Laura Morrow, eds, *Contemporary Literary Theory* (Macmillan: London 1989), p. 118.

10 Gordon Teskey, 'Allegory' in A. C. Hamilton *et al.*, eds, *The Spenser Encyclopaedia* (University of Toronto Press: Toronto and Buffalo, and Routledge, London 1990), pp. 16–22.

11 Roland Barthes, 'The Death of the Author' in *Image-Music-Text* (Fontana: Glasgow 1977), p. 148.

12 In the course of its own figurative interpretation of Abraham's two wives, Galatians 4 comments 'This is an allegory' (New English Bible, Galatians 4:24). The Greek word used here uniquely in the New Testament is *allegoroumena*: the Geneva translation is 'By the which things an other thing is meant'.

13 My translation of *Physiologus Latinus*, ed. Francis J. Carmody (Paris 1939), pp. 11–12.

14 My translation of Epistola 10, paragraph 7 in *Tutte le Opere di Dante Alighieri* ed. E. Moore (3rd edn, Oxford University Press: Oxford 1904), p. 415.

15 Dante, *The Divine Comedy: Purgatory* trans. Dorothy L. Sayers (Penguin: Harmondsworth 1955), canto II, 37–48.

16 Aristotle, *Poetics*, 1475.

17 Horace, *Satires*, I. i. 69–70.

18 Erasmus, *The Handbook of the Militant Christian* in *Essential Erasmus* selected and trans. John P. Dolan, (Mentor, New American Library: New York 1964), pp. 63–4.

19 For example, John Erskine Hankins, *Source and Meaning in Spenser's Allegory: A study of The Faerie Queene* (Clarendon Press: Oxford 1971), pp. 99–119; Josephine Waters Bennett, *The Evolution of the Faerie Queene* (University of Chicago Press: Chicago 1942), pp. 108–23; Florence Sandler, '*The Faerie Queene*: an Elizabethan apocalypse' in C. A. Patrides and Joseph Wittreich, eds, *The Apocalypse in English Renaissance Thought and Literature* (Manchester University Press: Manchester 1984), pp. 148–74. You may find the preceding five esssays in this book, on the interpretation of the Apocalypse up to the seventeenth century, interesting.

20 'Analogical', the relation of Old Testament to New or more widely the sense that draws a more general religious lesson, may be found less confusing than the alternative 'allegorical', which is also used as an inclusive term for all three mystical senses.

21 Robert Salter, *Wonderfull Prophecies* (1626), cited in Spenser, *Faerie Queene*, ed. Hamilton, p. 23.

Chapter 3 – Misreading

1 Umberto Eco, *A Theory of Semiotics* (Macmillan: London 1977), p. 7.

2 Hamilton, p. 44.

3 Abraham Fraunce, *The Arcadian Rhetorike* (1588), Chapter 7, sig. Bv.

4 With Una's veil compare Roland Barthes's idea of the sign which conveys both meaning and how that meaning is produced. This he regards as more healthy than the sign which disguises itself and passes itself off as natural, thus masking its signifying process.

5 Probably the most famous instances are Puttenham's reference to 'a new company of courtly makers' springing up in the latter part of Henry VIII's reign (*Arte of English Poesie* ed. Gladys Doidge Willcock

and Alice Walker (Cambridge University Press: Cambridge 1936), p. 60) and Sidney's comment that 'whether by luck or wisdom, we Englishmen have met with the Greeks in calling him [sc. a poet] "a maker"' (*An Apology for Poetry*, ed. Geoffrey Shepherd (Manchester University Press 1973, p. 99)).

6 Puttenham, *Arte* p. 154.

7 Ibid., p. 186.

8 Gayatari C. Spivack, translator's preface to Jacques Derrida, *Of Grammatology* (Johns Hopkins University Press: Baltimore, MD 1976), cited by Danny J. Anderson, 'Deconstruction: critical strategy/ strategic criticism' in G. Douglas Atkins and Laura Morrow, eds, *Contemporary Literary Theory* (Macmillan, 1989), p. 140.

9 Puttenham, *Arte*, p. 189. Quintilian described irony as capable of colouring a whole discourse pronounced in a tone of voice which does not correspond to the situation. This is noted by Paul de Mann in 'The rhetoric of temporality' in *Blindness and Insight: Essays in the rhetoric of contemporary criticism* (2nd edn, University of Minnesota Press: Minneapolis 1983), pp. 187–228. De Mann's essay is difficult but suggests some fascinating relationships between allegory, symbol and irony.

10 For some of the general issues raised here see 'Reading as a Woman' in Jonathan Culler, *On Deconstruction: Theory and criticism after structuralism* (Routledge and Kegan Paul: London 1983), 43–64.

11 Thomas Brightman, *The Revelation of St John Illustrated*, cited by Bernard Capp, 'The Political Dimension of Apocalyptic Thought' in C. A. Patrides and J. Wittreich, eds, *The Apocalypse in English Renaissance Thought and Literature* (Manchester University Press: Manchester 1984), p. 93.

12 See Simon Shepherd, *Spenser* (Harvester Wheatsheaf: Hemel Hempstead 1989), esp. pp. 58–60.

13 On Elizabeth as addressee of the poem and the related issue of the gendered reader of *The Faerie Queene*, see Maureen Quilligan, *Milton's Spenser: the politics of reading* (Cornell University Press: Ithaca 1983), esp. pp. 37–41, 179–85.

14 For details of changes in this list of addressees in successive issues of the 1590 edition see Penguin edition, pp. 1072–5.

15 Here I follow the general argument of Sandra M. Gilbert and Susan Gubar, *The Madwoman in the Attic: the woman writer and the nineteenth-century imagination*, (Yale University Press: New Haven 1979) 3–44. Gilbert and Gubar use Una and Duessa as specific examples in their argument, pp. 29–33.

Chapter 4 – Structure and Narrative in Book I

1 A. C. Hamilton concisely surveys the field in his introduction to Book I, *The Faerie Queene*, ed. Hamilton (Longman: London and New York), pp. 23–26. A digest of some critical approaches to Book I's narrative up to 1932, including the St George story and possible allusions to persons and events in the sixteenth century, may be sampled in *The Works of Edmund Spenser: A Variorum Edition. The Faerie Queene Book I*, ed. Edwin Greenlaw, Charles Grosvenor

Osgood and Frederick Morgan Padelford (Johns Hopkins University Press: Baltimore, MD 1932), appendices IV to VI, pp. 379–495. For ideas about Book I and numerological structure see Alastair Fowler, *Spenser and the Numbers of Time* (Routledge and Kegan Paul: London 1964), esp. pp. 63–79; for Protestant theological doctrines Virgil K. Whitaker, 'The Theological Structure of *Faerie Queene* Book I' in Hamilton, ed., *Essential Articles for the Study of Edmund Spenser* (Archon Books: Hamden, CT 1972), pp. 101–12; for Protestant versions of Church history see Frank Kermode, '*The Faerie Queene*, I and V' in *Shakespeare, Spenser, Donne* (Routledge and Kegan Paul 1971), pp. 33–59, esp. pp. 39–49.

2 A. C. Hamilton on stanzas 43–45 in the Longman edition.

3 Milton, *Paradise Lost*, IX. 28–37.

4 For example, in any of a series of books by Roy Strong: *Portraits of Elizabeth I* (Oxford University Press: London 1963); *The Cult of Elizabeth: Elizabethan portraiture and pageantry* (Thames and Hudson: London 1977); *The English Renaissance Miniature* (Thames and Hudson: London: 1983).

5 A brief account may be gleaned from either Hamilton's notes on these stanzas or the Variorum edition Vol. 1, pp. 284–6.

6 Augustine, *Enchiridion ad Laurentium: sive de fide, spe et charitate* Book I, chapter xi, in *Patrologiae cursus completus* series Latina, ed. J. P. Migne, Vol. 40 (Paris 1887), column 236.

7 Jonson, 'Timber: or Discoveries' in *Complete Poems* ed. G. Parfitt (Penguin: Harmondsworth 1975), p. 405.

8 A closer and more literal translation of this maxim than Wilson's is even more relevant to the imagery of *Faerie Queene*, Book I: 'Opposites placed together shine out more brightly'.

9 Thomas Wilson, *Arte of Rhetoric* (1553) f.69 [ed. Thomas J. Derrick (Garland: New York and London 1982), p. 257].

10 Quintilian, *Institutio oratoria*, 1.6.34.

11 Peacham, *Garden of Eloquence*, sig C4v.

12 Quintilian. *Institutio oratoria* 8.6.44.

13 A. Bartlett Giamatti, *Play of Double Senses: Spenser's Faerie Queene* (Englewood Cliffs, NJ 1975; reprint Norton, New York 1990). The title borrows from III.iv.28.7–8, 'subtile sophismes which do play/ With double senses'.

Chapter 5 – Temperate Reading

1 Cited in *Edmund Spenser: A Critical Anthology*, ed. Paul J. Alpers (Penguin: Harmondsworth 1969) p. 159.

2 C. S. Lewis, *The Allegory of Love: A Study in Medieval Tradition* (Clarendon Press: Oxford 1936), p. 353.

3 Sir Thomas Elyot, *The Book Named the Governor* (1531), ed. S. E. Lehmberg (Everyman: London 1962), p. 39.

4 Aristotle, *The Nicomachean Ethics*, trans. David Ross (World's Classics, Oxford University Press: Oxford 1980), 1109[a], pp. 45–6. This edition's translation of Homer has been replaced with that in *The Odyssey* trans. Walter Shewring (World's Classics, Oxford University Press: Oxford and New York 1980).

5 C. S. Lewis, *English Literature in the Sixteenth Century Excluding Drama* (Clarendon Press: Oxford 1954), p. 384.
6 Terry Eagleton, *Literary Theory: an Introduction* (Blackwell: Oxford 1983), p. 77.

Chapter 6 – Reading for Pleasure

1 Homer, *The Odyssey*, trans. Walter Shewring (Oxford University Press: Oxford 1980).
2 George Sandys, *Ovid's Metamorphosis. Englished, Mythologized and Represented in Figures* (1632) ed. Karl K. Hulley and Stanley T. Vandersall (University of Nebraska Press: Lincoln, 1970), p. 646.
3 Letter to Ralegh (*Faerie Queene*, Penguin edn, p. 15).
4 Milton, *Areopagitica* (1644) in *Edmund Spenser: A Critical Anthology*, ed. Paul J. Alpers (Penguin: Harmondsworth 1969), p. 62.
5 The remarks are those of William Hazlitt (1818), James Russell Lowell (1875), Edward Dowden (1882) and W. B. Yeats (1902). All these comments, and longer extracts from the essays which contain them can be usefully found collected in *Edmund Spenser. A Critical Anthology* ed. Paul J. Alpers (Penguin: Harmondsworth 1969), pp. 131–2, 156–8, 164–5, 174]. This paperback is very useful as in its sequence of extracts from critics it provides a brief sketch of critical taste for and response to Spenser from his contemporaries to the 1960s.
6 George Bornstein 'Yeats' in A. C. Hamilton *et al.*, eds, *The Spenser Encyclopaedia* (University of Toronto Press: Toronto and Buffalo, and Routledge: London 1990), p. 739.
7 Sir Herbert J. C. Grierson, *Cross Currents in English Literature of the XVIIth Century* (Chatto and Windus: London 1929), pp. 53–4.
8 C. S. Lewis, 'The Faerie Queene' is Chapter VII in *The Allegory of Love* (Oxford University Press: Oxford 1936), pp. 297–360. The particular argument about the Bower is at pp. 321–33; extracts in Hamilton, ed., *Essential Articles for the Study of Edmund Spenser* (Archon Books: Hamden, CT 1972), pp. 3–12 and Alpers, *Spenser: A Critical Anthology*, pp. 190–210.
9 Stephen Greenblatt, 'To Fashion a Gentleman: Spenser and the destruction of the Bower of Bliss' in *Renaissance Self-fashioning* (University of Chicago Press: Chicago and London 1980), pp. 157–92; B. Nellist, 'The Allegory of Guyon's Voyage', *English Literary History*, 30 (1963) 89–106; Brooke's reply to Lewis (1949) and Ruth Nevo 'Spenser's "Bower of Bliss" and a Key Metaphor from Renaissance Poetic' are all in Hamilton, *Essential Articles*. A selection of others are listed by Hamilton in the Longman edition of *Faerie Queene*, p. 168.
10 *Metamorphoses*, IV. 604ff. The verse translation by A. D. Melville (World's Classics, Oxford University Press: Oxford 1987) is good.
11 Sir John Harington, 'A Brief Apology of Poetry' prefaced to his translation of Ariosto, *Orlando Furioso* (1591).
12 *The Merchant of Venice* (Penguin edn), I.iii.99.
13 Sidney, *An Apology for Poetry*, ed. Geoffrey Shepherd (Manchester University Press: Manchester 1973), p. 102.

14 Ibid., pp. 123–5, 103.
15 Ibid., p. 113.
16 Baldassare Castiglione, *The Book of the Courtier*, trans. Sir Thomas Hoby (1561) Book IV (Everyman edn, Dent: London 1974, p. 265).
17 Émile Legouis, *Spenser*, (Dent: London and Toronto 1926), p. 137.

Chapter 7 – Romance

1 Cited by Caroline Lucas, *Writing for Women: the example of woman as reader in Elizabethan romance* (Open University Press: Milton Keynes 1989), p. 40.
2 Thomas Tallis's motet, *Spem in Alium* ('Hope in another . . .').
3 Byrd's 'Mass in Five Parts' provides a sacred example. A pair of records (OUP 151/2) was made to accompany Philip Ledger, ed., *The Oxford Book of English Madrigals* (Oxford University Press: Oxford 1978). On this recording, John Bennet's 'Weep, O Mine Eyes' and John Ward's 'Come, Sable Night' provide examples of the polyphonic expression of the pains of love which are interesting comparisons with both the form and the subject matter of Book III.
4 Ariosto, *Orlando Furioso* trans. Sir John Harington (1607 edn: originally 1591) I.13 and I.33–5.
5 To be strictly accurate, 'kid of bearded goate' is an embellishment or mistake in Harington's translation. Ariosto has 'Like a young deer or roebuck doe *(capriuola)*'.
6 An illuminating comparison would be the figure of Spenser's forester with the images, language and unrelieved drive of Shakespeare's sonnet 128, 'An expense of spirit in a waste of shame'.
7 Petrarch, *Familiares*, XXIII.19, cited and translated in Nicholas Mann, *Petrarch* (Oxford University Press: Oxford 1984), p. 19.
8 The most easily available translation is Ariosto, *Orlando Furioso*, trans. by Barbara Reynolds, 2 vols (Penguin: Harmondsworth 1975 and 1977).
9 Chris Baldick, *The Concise Oxford Dictionary of Literary Terms* (Oxford University Press: Oxford 1990), 191.
10 Gillian Beer, *The Romance* (Methuen: London 1970), pp. 5, 10.
11 The excellent article on *romance* by Patricia Parker in A. C. Hamilton *et al.*, eds, *The Spenser Encyclopaedia* (University of Toronto Press: Toronto and Buffalo, and Routledge, London 1990), pp. 609–18, is difficult to better for its concision in summary and relevance to Spenser, and the bibliography at its end will direct you to further reading. The details of Gillian Beer's book on romance are given in the previous footnote.
12 Gilbert Highet, *The Classical Tradition: Greek and Roman influences on Western literature* (Clarendon Press: Oxford 1949, reprinted 1967), p. 140.
13 Beer, *The Romance*, p. 10.

Chapter 8 – 'Endlesse Worke'

1 Petrarch *Rime Sparse* 157, lines 9–14, from *Petrarch's Lyric Poems. The Rime Sparse and other lyrics* trans. and ed. Robert M. Durling

(Harvard University Press: Cambridge, MA and London, 1976), p. 335.

2 Thomas Watson, *Hekatompathia* (1582), poem 7, lines 1–4 and 9–11, quoted in Shakespeare, *The Sonnets and A Lover's Complaint*, ed. John Kerrigan (Penguin: Harmondsworth 1986), p. 19.

3 Petrarch, Sonnet 189 'Passe la nave mia' in *Petrarch's Lyric Poems*, p. 335.

4 Wyatt, 'My galley charged with forgetfulness' in *Sir Thomas Wyatt. The Complete Poems*, ed. R.A. Rebholz (Penguin: Harmondsworth 1978), p. 81.

5 *Hamlet*, ed T. J. B. Spencer, introduction by Anne Barton (Penguin: Harmondsworth 1980), p. 54.

6 A. C. Hamilton's note on iv.8–10 in Faerie Queene, Longman edition, p. 337.

7 A letter from Spenser's friend Gabriel Harvey records that Spenser wished to emulate and 'overgo' *Orlando Furioso*. The relevant passage from Harvey's letter is given in *Edmund Spenser: A Critical Anthology*, ed. Paul J. Alpers (Penguin: Harmondsworth 1969) p. 37.

Suggestions for Further Reading

There is an enormous number of books on Spenser, and the following list is necessarily highly selective. I have tried first to suggest what might be most useful as the next steps in helping you to read the *Faerie Queene*. In addition to references in the notes to individual chapters, I conclude by listing, by chapter, articles and books which might be of interest to readers wishing to follow up specific points which emerge in these chapters, as well as some general books on Spenser.

Editions

I have recommended *The Faerie Queene*, ed. Thomas P. Roche Jr (Penguin: Harmondsworth 1978) as the most easily available, as reasonably priced and as physically manageable. *The Faerie Queene*, ed. A. C. Hamilton (Longman: London and New York 1977) is excellent and recommended for serious students of Spenser's poem. However, like other very fully annotated editions of literary works, this one may slow first readers down, and the erudition of the annotations may intimidate readers who are still getting used to the poem and its complexities. Hamilton's summaries, at the beginning of each book of the poem, of critical issues and of relevant criticism are especially good. *The Works of Spenser: A Variorum Edition*, ed. Edwin Greenlaw *et al.*, 11 vols (Johns Hopkins University Press: Baltimore, MD 1932–57) is copiously annotated and useful for its long extracts from annotation and criticism up to 1957. It will be found only in university and large public libraries.

Bibliographies

Sufficiently full bibliographies can be found at the end of Hamilton's edition (pp. 745–53) and at the end of the *Spenser Encyclopaedia* (pp. 790–809, see below). There is also Waldo McNeir and Foster Provost, *Edmund Spenser: an annotated bibliography* (Harvester Press: Brighton 1975)

Critical Anthologies

There are several of these: the best is probably A. C. Hamilton, ed., *Essential Articles for the Study of Edmund Spenser* (Archon Books: Hamden, CT 1972). Also worth consulting are: Paul J. Alpers, ed., *Edmund Spenser: a critical anthology* (Penguin: Harmondsworth 1969); Harry Berger Jr, *Spenser: A collection of critical essays* (Prentice Hall: Englewood Cliffs, NJ 1968); *Critical Essays on Spenser from 'ELH'* (Johns Hopkins University Press: Baltimore MD 1970); John R. Elliott Jr, ed., *The Prince of Poets: essays on Edmund Spenser* (University of London Press: London 1968); R. M. Cummings, ed., *Spenser: the critical heritage* (Routledge and Kegan Paul: London 1971). Hamilton, Berger and *Critical Essays on Spenser from 'ELH'* collect modern essays; Alpers, Elliott and Cummings make available useful extracts from critics of Spenser from earlier centuries, and it is from anthologies like these I have usually quoted the comments of readers from the sixteenth to nineteenth centuries.

Mention must also be made of A. C. Hamilton, Donald Cheney, W. F. Blisset, David A. Richardson and William W. Barker, eds, *The Spenser Encyclopaedia* (University of Toronto Press: Toronto and Buffalo, and Routledge: London 1990). This enormous and extraordinarily detailed book took most of a decade in its preparation. It is good not only for the entries on detailed aspects of the *Faerie Queene* but also for excellent concentrated articles on enormous subjects in the culture of the Renaissance (such as 'humanism' and 'Platonism'). I found the articles on 'allegory' and 'romance' excellent, and there is an elegant and comprehensive piece on Book II. Since part of the aim of the *Encyclopaedia* is to sum up the current state of scholarship on Spenser, and it does this so successfully, there is a danger that it might replace the poem for readers who want a quick survey or digest of an aspect of the *Faerie Queene*. You are likely to find it only in university libraries. I have the same reservations about Douglas Brooks-Davies, *Spenser's Faerie Queene: a critical commentary on Books I and II* (Manchester University Press: Manchester 1977) as about *The Spenser Encyclopaedia* and feel the annotations overinterpret the poem in too schematic a way.

In the way of books to read next, I suggest the following as particularly suited to new readers of the poem: A. Bartlett Giamatti, *Play of Double Senses: Spenser's Faerie Queene* (Prentice Hall: Englewood Cliffs, NJ 1975, reissued 1991); Rosemary Freeman, *The Faerie Queene: a companion for readers* (Chatto and Windus: London 1970), A. C. Hamilton, *The Structure of Allegory in The Faerie Queene* (Clarendon Press: Oxford 1961), Elizabeth Heale, *The Faerie Queene: a reader's guide* (Cambridge University Press: Cambridge 1987), Humphrey Tonkin, *The Faerie Queene* (Unwin Critical Library: London 1988).

Other books on the *Faerie Queene* are: John Erskine Hankins, *Source and Meaning in Spenser's Allegory* (Clarendon Press: Oxford 1971); Harry Berger Jr, *Revisionary Play: studies in the Spenserian dynamics* (University of California Press: Berkeley, Los Angeles and London 1988), the first half of which contains several essays on Book III; Paul J. Alpers, *The Poetry of the Faerie Queene* (Princeton University Press: Princeton, NJ 1967); Donald Cheney, *Spenser's Image of Nature:*

wild man and shepherd in the Faerie Queene (Yale University Press: New Haven, CT 1966); Angus Fletcher, *The Prophetic Moment: an essay on Spenser* (University of Chicago Press: Chicago 1971); Graham Hough, *A Preface to the Faerie Queene* (Duckworth: London 1962); James Nohrnberg, *The Analogy of the Faerie Queene* (Princeton University Press: Princeton, NJ 1976), a large and dauntingly erudite book; Michael O'Connell, *Mirror and Veil: the historical dimension of Spenser's Faerie Queene* (University of North Carolina Press: Chapel Hill, NC 1977); and Isabel MacCaffrey, *Spenser's Allegory: the anatomy of imagination* (Princeton University Press: Princeton, NJ 1976).

Follow-up Reading

Chapter 1
Some detailed analyses of the Error episode are listed in note 10 to this chapter.

Chapter 2
Angus Fletcher, *Allegory: the theory of a symbolic mode* (Cornell University Press: Ithaca, NY 1964); Michael Murrin, *The Veil of Allegory: some notes toward a theory of allegorical rhetoric in the English Renaissance* (University of Chicago Press: Chicago 1969); and Rosemund Tuve, *Allegorical Imagery: some medieval books and their posterity* (Princeton University Press: Princeton, NJ 1966).

Chapter 3
Anthea Hume, *Edmund Spenser: Protestant poet* (Cambridge University Press: Cambridge 1984).

Chapter 4
William J. Kennedy, 'Rhetoric, Allegory and Dramatic Modality in Spenser's Fradubio Episode', *English Literary Renaissance*, 3 (1973) 351–68; and Mary R. Bowman, ' "She there as Princess rained": Spenser's Figures of Elizabeth', *Renaissance Quarterly*, 43 (1990) 509–28.

Chapter 5
Harry Berger Jr, *The Allegorical Temper: vision and reality in Book II of Spenser's Faerie Queene* (Yale University Press: New Haven 1957); Ernest Sirluck, 'The *Faerie Queene* Book II and the *Nicomachean Ethics*', *Modern Philology*, 49 (1952) 73–100; Don Cameron Allen, *Mysteriously Meant: the rediscovery of pagan symbolism and allegorical interpretation in the Renaissance* (Johns Hopkins University Press: Baltimore, MD 1970); B. Nellist, 'The Allegory of Guyon's Voyage', *English Literary History*, 30 (1963) 89–106.

Chapter 6
Extracts from C. S. Lewis on the subject of the Bower of Bliss, a reply by N. S. Brooke, 'C. S. Lewis and Spenser: nature, art and the Bower of Bliss', and two other articles, Robert M. Durling, 'The Bower of Bliss and Armida's Palace' and Ruth Nevo 'Spenser's "Bower of Bliss" and a Key

Metaphor from Renaissance Poetic' are all in Hamilton, *Essential Articles*. See also A. Bartlett Giamatti, *The Earthly Paradise and the Renaissance Epic* (Princeton University Press: Princeton, NJ) , esp. pp. 232–90; and Merritt Y. Hughes, 'Spenser's Acrasia and the Circe of the Renaissance', *Journal of the History of Ideas*, 4 (1943) 381–99.

Chapter 7
Caroline Lucas, *Writing for Women: the example of woman as reader in Elizabethan romance* (Open University Press: Milton Keynes 1989); John Arthos, *On the Poetry of Spenser and the Form of Romances* (Allen and Unwin: London 1956); William Blisset, 'Florimell and Marinell', *Studies in English Literature 1500–1900*, 5 (1965) 87–104; Graham Hough, *A Preface to the Faerie Queene*, esp. 1–47; Thomas P. Roche Jr, *The Kindly Flame: a study of the Faerie Queene III and IV* (Princeton University Press: Princeton, NJ 1964).

Chapter 8
J. S. Weld 'The Complaint of Britomart: word-play and symbolism', *Publications of the Modern Language Association*, 66 (1951) 548–51; Kathleen Williams, 'Spenser: some uses of the sea and the storm-tossed ship', *Research Opportunities in Renaissance Drama*, 13–14 (1970–1) 135–42. Jerome S. Dees, 'The Ship Conceit in the *Faerie Queene*: "conspicuous allusion" and poetic structure', *Studies in Philology*, 72 (1975) 208–25.

Kathleen Williams, 'Venus and Diana: some uses of myth in the *Faerie Queene*' in Hamilton, *Essential Articles*, pp. 202–19; Judith H. Anderson, ' "In Liuing Colours and Right Hew": The Queen of Spenser's Central Books' in Maynard Mack and George deForest Lord, eds, *Poetic Traditions of the English Renaissance* (Yale University Press: New Haven, CT 1982), pp. 47–66; John B. Bender, *Spenser and Literary Pictorialism* (Princeton University Press: Princeton, NJ 1972).

Stevie Davies, *The Idea of Woman in Renaissance Literature: the feminine reclaimed* (Harvester: Brighton 1986); Linda Woodbridge, *Women and the English Renaissance* (Harvester: Brighton 1984); Maureen Quilligan, *Milton's Spenser: the politics of reading* (Cornell University Press: Ithaca and London 1983); Joan Kelly-Gadol, 'Early Feminist Theory and the *Querelle des femmes* 1400–1789', *Signs*, 8 (Autumn 1982); Joan Kelly-Gadol, 'Did women have a Renaissance?' in Renate Bridenthal and Claudia Koonz, eds, *Becoming Visible: women in European history* (Houghton Mifflin: Boston 1977) pp. 139–64; Lauren Silberman, 'Singing Unsung Heroines: androgynous discourse in Book 3 of *The Faerie Queene*' in Margaret W. Ferguson, Maureen Quilligan and Nancy J. Vickers, eds, *Rewriting the Renaissance: the discourses of sexual difference in early modern Europe* (University of Chicago Press: Chicago and London 1986), pp. 259–71.

Donald Cheney, 'Spenser's Hermaphrodite and the 1590 *Faerie Queene*', *Publications of the Modern Language Association*, 87 (1972) 192–200; Albert R. Cirillo, 'The Fair Hermaphrodite: love-union in the poetry of Donne and Spenser', *Studies in English Literature 1500–1900*, 9 (1969), 81–95.

Index